ROOM by ROOM:

KITCHENS

ROOM by ROOM:

KITCHENS

YOUR HOUSE MADE SIMPLE

Lillian Hayes Martin

STERLING

New York / London
www.sterlingpublishing.com

STERLING and the distinctive Sterling logo are registered trademarks of Sterling Publishing Co., Inc.

Library of Congress Cataloging-in-Publication Data

Martin, Lillian Hayes.
 Room by room : kitchens : your home made simple / Lillian Hayes Martin.
   p. cm.
 Includes index.
 ISBN-13: 978-1-4027-2893-8
 ISBN-10: 1-4027-2893-X
 1. Kitchens. 2. Home economics. I. Title. II. Title: Kitchens : your home made simple.

NK2117.K5M33 2008
643.3--dc22
                          2007048105

10 9 8 7 6 5 4 3 2 1

Published by Sterling Publishing Co., Inc.
387 Park Avenue South, New York, NY 10016
© 2008 by Sterling Publishing Co., Inc.
Distributed in Canada by Sterling Publishing
c/o Canadian Manda Group, 165 Dufferin Street
Toronto, Ontario, Canada M6K 3H6
Distributed in the United Kingdom by GMC Distribution Services
Castle Place, 166 High Street, Lewes, East Sussex, England BN7 1XU
Distributed in Australia by Capricorn Link (Australia) Pty. Ltd.
P.O. Box 704, Windsor, NSW 2756, Australia

Series developed by Pam Liflander
Packaged by LightSpeed Publishing, Inc.
Interior design by X-Height Studio

Sterling ISBN-13: 978-1-4027-2893-8
        ISBN-10: 1-4027-2893-X

For information about custom editions, special sales, premium
and corporate purchases, please contact Sterling Special Sales
Department at 800-805-5489 or specialsales@sterlingpublishing.com.

Contents

CHAPTER 9

Cooking Techniques Everyone Needs to Know 181

Introduction

The kitchen, where many of us spend so much time, is often the biggest disappointment of the home. When I ask people to describe their kitchen, I repeatedly hear, "It's too small," "It has no storage," "It's ugly," "It's old," or "It's brand new but not my style." Unfortunately, most of these comments are on target. I've seen my fair share of kitchens, and usually the words "terrible," "ugly," and "dysfunctional" come to mind.

My first house had faux wood countertops. Let me tell you, no one was fooled! I wouldn't even move into the house until we gutted it. Unfortunately, instead of enjoying my new kitchen, as soon as the construction was finished, my family had to relocate. In our new town, all we could afford was a charming, albeit old, cottage. In phase one of Operation Salvage (nothing more than pressure washing), water started seeping through the baseboards as I stood in the kitchen. And then there was an electrical fire caused by the refrigerator, which was on an extension cord. That kitchen had to go as well. All in all, I've lived in seven different kitchens, and renovated three homes in three different cities. I've had an art deco kitchen, a funky cottage kitchen, and I'm just finishing my latest—a modern kitchen with an organic twist.

Now that the dust has settled, and as we unpack the china and silverware that's been in storage for six months, we're slowly getting to appreciate the work that's been done. Our kitchen is showing off a bit with shiny new surfaces and well-lit interiors. The kids have found the snack shelf in the pantry and

I've decided to stop torturing my husband and leave the drawers alone at night so that he can actually find a spoon for breakfast. Hopefully, this will be my last kitchen renovation, but you never know!

The Four P's

Why do I love my new kitchen? There is a place for everything and everyone. But it wasn't by accident. When I designed the space, I followed my motto of "the four P's"—proper planning prevents problems. I thought long and hard about what problems I needed to solve. For example, I noticed that when one cabinet door was shut, another one opened. No, it wasn't a poltergeist—the cabinets were original to the house and couldn't be fixed. And I could never fit my cookie sheets into the pint-sized wall oven. So I had to add a new range to my wish list. Discoveries like these made it easier to make the right decisions during the renovation.

You too can have the kitchen of your dreams. Whether you're ready to start all over, trying to pick a wall color, or simply shopping for a new microwave, this book can help you formulate a plan of attack. Armed with the proper knowledge, you will be able to solve or prevent many of the typical issues that arise in every household. By analyzing your cooking style, your decorating tastes, and your shopping habits, you can truly transform your kitchen and learn to use it more effectively.

The most important part of planning is to make sure your kitchen reflects who you are and how your family operates. For example, do you have too little cabinet space or too much stuff? Do you strain your back getting the omelet pan every morning? Having easy access to the things you use most is all about organization and placement. By making sure that everyone's needs will be met, my new kitchen suits our entire family.

Functional Living

There is a subtle art to setting up a kitchen that functions to its fullest capacity. As the mother of two sons, fullest capacity is when my older son sits at the kitchen island doing homework while the younger one is careening madly, circling the room. Meanwhile, I'm prepping, chopping, following a recipe, fielding questions and phone calls, and my husband is shrieking "hot off the grill!"

Whether or not your lifestyle mirrors mine (and peace be with you if it does), more and more people are asking their kitchens to be the hub of the family compound. Maybe you love to entertain big groups and cook everything from scratch. Or maybe your kitchen functions as a room where you heat up instant coffee in the morning and serve take-out meals at night. This book is all about making the most of your kitchen: how to arrange it better, keep it cleaner, and create efficiencies so that you can enjoy the rest of your day.

How This Book Works

This book will serve as the Community Answers for your kitchen. In the ensuing pages, I've included everything you'll need to know to set up a fabulous kitchen that not only meets your needs but provides a comfortable space for the entire family to enjoy.

Like cars, kitchens are expensive to purchase, filled with complicated equipment, and outdated quickly by new technology. The first three chapters tackle the difficult questions that arise when you want to redesign, update, or redecorate your kitchen. Kitchens run the gamut of the design spectrum. Some people open their kitchen walls to create a larger family room while others prefer a separate space that is the domain of a more serious chef. If you are lucky, you're in a home where the kitchen décor fits seamlessly into the style of the rest of the house. Most likely, though, it clashes, and you're stuck with dated colors and unaesthetic appliances from a past decade. When you are designing a new kitchen, or even making the smallest renovations, it's easy to get frustrated. With so many downsides, it's no wonder that many people try to get by with what they have for as long as possible.

Once you do decide to change your kitchen, you'll want help to plan and execute your dreams. Most people consider enlisting the help of a professional: either an independent kitchen designer or someone who works for a home improvement center. A good designer will focus on the needs of your household and create a plan that works for you. But even when you use a professional, it's too expensive an undertaking to leave all the decisions up to someone else.

The first chapter in this book will teach you about space planning, layout, and design. There are specific elements that make up every kitchen, from countertops to flooring options. Chapter 1 will also help you choose a décor that fits your house and lifestyle preferences. By addressing your lifestyle choices in a worksheet format, you can narrow down your personal preferences, saving time and money.

Part of designing a successful kitchen is to integrate the right appliances into the floor plan. Purchasing appliances is a large portion of any budget so it's important to be a well-informed consumer. Chapter 2 addresses the smartest way to choose appliances, both big and small, including information on what makes them different from one another in both cost and energy efficiency.

Once your kitchen is designed to your liking, you'll want to fill it with the best tools. Any professional chef will tell you that cooking success lies largely in the equipment. In chapter 3, we sift through the myriad of tools and equipment available and help you focus on where to spend your money.

The next couple of chapters focus on "living." You'll discover how to really work, play, and enjoy yourself in your kitchen. After all, the kitchen is a room where you will spend a great deal of your time. Wouldn't it be great for it to be organized, running at full capacity, and a pleasant space to inhabit?

Are you constantly running out of milk? Do you strain your back getting the table set? Do you wake up with your fingers crossed that the dishwasher works? You'll learn how to clear the clutter and reorganize your kitchen to make it more efficient. In addition, you'll find more than the basics on keeping your kitchen clean, including useful information about maintaining your equipment.

Chapter 4 specifically outlines the tricks of the trade when it comes to organization. Perfect organization doesn't happen overnight. For example, when I got an electronic organizer, I thought it would be a great time-saver for grocery shopping.

The first time out, the battery died so I lost all my data! On the second run, I realized there was no way to tap my stylus, push the cart, control my three-year-old, and shop simultaneously. What did work, however, was using my organizer to jot down and generate a list that I could print and carry with me to the store.

Your kitchen is a place for self-expression—to whatever degree space and affordability will allow. Chapter 5 has practical, fun, and easy-to-complete projects and crafts. Depending upon the materials and colors you use, these projects can be as individualized as you are. You'll find it especially useful if you aren't interested in a full-blown renovation, just exciting ways to update your cabinets, add custom window treatments, refinish your floors, and make fun accessories that will be functional as well as conversation starters.

Once your kitchen is set up as you want it, it will be a snap to prepare great-tasting meals. But let's face it—the more you cook, the more you clean. Follow the steps outlined in chapter 6 to break down cleaning chores into a time-saving routine. The average family generates at least one or maybe two dishwashers full of dirty plates and utensils per day, and that doesn't count the cooking equipment used to produce the meals! So it makes sense to figure out the best way to get it all done.

In order for your kitchen to really function, you must be able to cook. The foods you choose have to keep well, be easy to reach, and ready to use at a moment's notice. Chapter 7 helps you plan your shopping trips, pick the freshest foods, and make the most of your cooking efforts. It doesn't matter if you are a working parent or an over-carpooled, volunteering homemaker, chapter 7 is all about saving money, time, and staying organized when you go shopping. You'll learn to pay attention to growing seasons and the best times to buy produce; you'll discover tips on clipping coupons, freezing meats, and how long you can expect your vegetables to stay fresh. You'll find out about alternative grocery outlets.

Determining where to put all that great food you bought is no easy feat since storage is at a premium in most households. In chapter 8, I've included everything you need to know about stocking your pantry so you'll be ready to follow any recipe. It's a complete guide to basic pantry items, from crackers to condiments to coffee. Topics regarding food safety and when you should splurge on organic ingredients are included to make you an informed consumer.

Ever go to a fancy restaurant, read a menu with a lustful gaze, and wish you knew how to cook like that? What's a demi-glaze? What's a reduction? Most restaurant chefs have been trained in classic French cooking techniques, which can seem intimidating to the home cook. Chapter 9 demonstrates that good cooking is really quite simple. It explains in plain language how to read a recipe and provides complete instructions for cooking techniques far beyond baking and broiling. We'll decode chefs' secrets of success, from braising, sautéing, and reducing to substituting ingredients and measuring accurately. With little effort, you'll be able to serve terrific new meals that your entire family will enjoy.

Once you're comfortable cooking, you'll naturally want to share your skills with family and friends. But no one wants to have an anxiety attack while planning a barbeque! Chapter 10 gives you the guts to go ahead and throw that party, whether or not your house is painted, decorated, or even clean! It begins with the basics, like creating a theme, and then lays out the differences between buffets and sit-down dinners. There are also lots of tips on lighting techniques, traffic flow, and how to create the perfect ambience. You'll find entertaining tips for every type of celebration, whether you are throwing a cocktail party, hosting a weekend barbeque, or serving a holiday meal.

Ultimately, *Room by Room: Kitchens* teaches you that your kitchen does not have to conform to anyone's standards but your own. If you feel queasy every time you walk into your kitchen, this book will show you how you can make the necessary changes and improvements to transform the room and have the kitchen you've always wanted, no matter your budget. Everything I have learned over the years is in this book. Whatever your goals are, your kitchen can be what you want it to be!

1

Designing Your Space

The ultimate goal *of good kitchen design is to create a room where you can cook, clean, and serve food with minimal effort. If your kitchen does not meet these basic requirements, it might be time to make a change. I don't expect you to put your home on the market and trade up for a new dwelling with a dream kitchen. Instead, I will show you exactly how to create the fabulous kitchen you've always wanted, right inside your own home.*

With that in mind, there's a saying my kids learned early on in school, and it's appropriate to repeat it now: "You get what you get, so don't get upset." Most people need to work within their existing kitchen's dimensions. Unless you're gutting your kitchen and starting from scratch, most of your existing kitchen, including the windows, doorways, and walls, will be staying in place. That's not to say that you wouldn't benefit from a bit of redesign by taking out a small closet or reworking an entrance. However, keep in mind that the steps you must take to improve an existing kitchen will always revolve around three things: money (how much you have to spend, knowing that kitchens are the most expensive room in the house to renovate), space (the area to work within), and function (making sure the kitchen operates according to your needs).

Basic Kitchen Design

A well-designed kitchen is as functional as it is beautiful. Kitchen projects must successfully combine personal preferences, cooking styles, and tastes, while adhering to basic design theories that have worked forever. But before you tear out the sink in disgust, it's best to take a deep breath and spend some time observing the actual comings and goings in your kitchen.

The first step to any major renovation project is to get yourself a spiral bound notebook and create a project log. Then, over the course of a week, jot down any observations that will help decide what will make your kitchen better. Begin by listing all the things in your kitchen that you don't like and asking yourself some basic questions. For example, do your kids bump hips near the refrigerator? If so, you might need a different style refrigerator door for the space. Do you find yourself screaming "Hot food!" while bodies scatter to get out of the way? Maybe the work area is too close to where the kids do their homework. Are your bills splattered with pasta sauce? Maybe you should consider a different prep area. Can someone answer the phone without disturbing the chef? Maybe you need to move the phone jack. Is it difficult to reach everyday dishes? Perhaps installing an under-counter plate rack would help.

Once you gather all your data, you'll find that some of these problems can be addressed with minor tweaking, and others may require major tweaking. For these, you'll decide how to live with them or what you can fix on your budget.

Next, find some quiet time to contemplate how your ideal kitchen would function. Consider how you want to use the kitchen space. Let yourself dream—but be forewarned. Dreams in reality can be nightmares. I had a friend who dreamed of a great room with an open kitchen only to find out that the blare of the kids' cartoons drove her crazy while she tried to read recipes. Kitchen remodeling has to take the needs of each family member into account. Therefore, the next step is to determine how your family will use a new and improved kitchen. Record your answers to the following questions in your project log. These will help you determine what the basic functional uses of your kitchen will be.

▪ Lifestyle Worksheet

How many people are in your household?

Who cooks and when?

Do you like to be alone when you cook or surrounded by friends and family?

Where do your kids do their homework?

Do you want to eat in the kitchen or in another more formal room?

Where do you currently pay bills?

Do you like displaying your stuff or do you like a room where everything is put away behind closed doors?

Do you want a computer, a television, or a telephone in the kitchen?

Do you have a library of cookbooks or a different sort of collection that you want to display?

Do you want to entertain frequently?

Do you shop for food in bulk? Where do you currently store these items?

Are there any special needs that must be taken into account, including disabilities or food allergies?

Can your children be self-sufficient in the kitchen or do you need to manage what they take to eat?

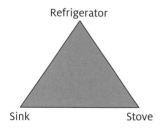

▲ **1.1** A "work triangle" includes the sink, stove, and refrigerator.

There are other fixed elements that need to be considered beyond how you intend to use your kitchen. The first is traffic flow, which is the natural progression of people as they cross back and forth performing various tasks. In a kitchen, above all else, people need to stay out of the chef's way. By observing the comings and goings of your existing kitchen traffic patterns, any problems will present themselves pretty quickly!

THE WORK TRIANGLE

Form follows function as the saying goes. Most kitchens house two groups of items: appliances and cabinetry. These should be laid out with a basic design that creates a "work triangle" that revolves around the placement of the sink, stove, and refrigerator, with cabinetry between them (**1.1**). Ideally, these elements should be near each other, in an area that is neither too big nor too small. The work triangle allows you to be more efficient in your movements while you cook.

Right now, count the steps from your sink to the refrigerator. It shouldn't be more than nine feet, with five or six feet being the average. If this space is bigger than nine feet, cooking becomes exhausting; too much smaller and you might feel like a chef in a submarine. Next, count the steps from the sink to the stove, and then from the stove to the refrigerator. The total shouldn't exceed 22 feet.

Don't panic. The work triangle is a theory! Many kitchens function just as well without it. If you haven't had a problem with your existing layout, it's probably just fine. Only you can be the judge of what works in your home.

Tried and True Kitchen Layouts

Obviously, the task of designing a space will change if you have a small kitchen or need to service many people. Most of these problems can be solved by figuring out a basic configuration for the space, and then addressing the current layout problems. This brings us to the next question: When exactly was your kitchen built?

Modern kitchens emphasize different appliances than previous generations. If your kitchen was built before the invention of the microwave, chances are its placement was an afterthought and can be improved. Let's face it—people use their microwave every day, if not several times for each meal. They probably use it more than the oven! Centralizing the location of the microwave instead of the oven might just make sense for your family. (See chapter 2 for just how great new microwaves are!)

Because of new kitchen innovations, the layout that worked in a 1930's home might not work today. What follows are some of the most common kitchen designs. Read through all of them before deciding which one is best for you. If your kitchen doesn't follow one of these patterns, then you have to decide if you want to change something that is truly unique.

THE ONE-ROW KITCHEN

This basic layout features the kitchen appliances, cabinets, and storage grouped together along one wall (**1.2**). Often found in a small apartment, its restrictions are obvious. There is usually room for only one person at a time. Storage is limited. When purchasing appliances for a one-row kitchen, mini-versions are typical. On the positive side, if you have a one-row layout within a larger room, the entire kitchen area can be easily concealed behind a screen or a curtain and completely hidden when not in use.

THE TWO-ROW KITCHEN

Also known as a Galley, Gallery, Corridor, or Pullman (like the train car) kitchen, this layout is a long space that is closed in by two walls, with the appliances and cabinets on both sides facing each other (**1.3**). A corridor kitchen can be entered by both of the open sides or only one. Usually, but not necessarily, the width is enough for two people to pass without touching

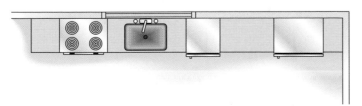

◀ 1.2 The one-row kitchen is a very basic layout.

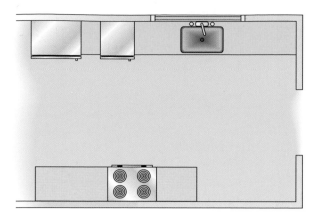

▶ **1.3** The two-row kitchen is also a very popular design.

each other. Wall cut-outs or pass-throughs to other rooms are common ways to open up the space.

AN ISLAND KITCHEN

Gaining in popularity, an island kitchen is basically a two-row kitchen in which a freestanding island replaces one of the walls (**1.4**). It is also common as part of a great room configuration where the kitchen island separates a sitting or gathering area. The island directs traffic away from the work triangle and provides counter space on the interior side and eating options on the other side. This design offers a true workhorse of a kitchen. The kids can snack and do homework, or your guests can sip wine and nibble on hors d'oeuvres while you prep dinner unencumbered on the other side.

▶ **1.4** An island kitchen provides usable space away from the work triangle.

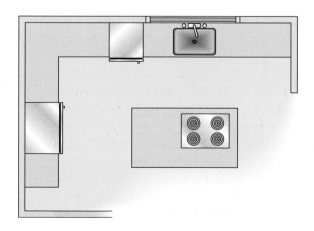

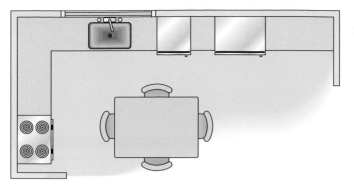

◀ **1.5** An L-shaped kitchen is good if your design includes a kitchen table.

Can an island fit in your kitchen? Ideally, it should be at least three and half feet from the edge of the outer counters. The island itself can be as small as two feet square but three feet is more functional. It can also have a different surface than the rest of your kitchen, or can be placed on wheels to roll out when you need a larger space. If you are not sure if you would enjoy an island design, skip to chapter 5 for instructions on building your own island to see if it would work for you.

THE L-SHAPED KITCHEN

Shaped like the letter L, the kitchen may or may not have an island or a peninsula. However, an L-shaped kitchen has the appliances and cabinetry located on two adjoining walls. This design works well if you would like to incorporate a kitchen table within your kitchen (**1.5**). The table can be placed in the center of the L.

THE U-SHAPED KITCHEN

Shaped like the letter U, this layout works quite efficiently. Usually the refrigerator, sink, and stove are on separate walls and the very nature of its shape makes traffic flow well (**1.6**). By introducing an island in a larger U-shaped kitchen, you can create a great workspace for a second cook, or a counter space for serving food. U-shaped kitchens are ideal if you require a lot of concealed storage space: you'll have plenty of cabinets and surface area to work with.

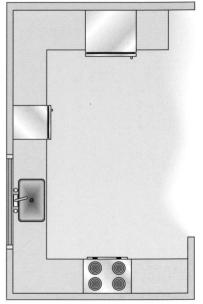

▲ **1.6** U-shaped kitchens provide plenty of hidden storage space.

A Word About Small Kitchens

Don't think for a minute you have to suffer because your kitchen is the size of another friend's walk-in closet. A small kitchen can be an efficient, hardworking space. Banish any activities, such as sorting the mail, to another area. If possible, store seldom-used items, like grandma's china, in the dining room. Consider using open shelving on top, which will force you to be neater and purge unused equipment. Invest in cabinet organizers and watch as your storage potential skyrockets.

TOP KITCHEN LAYOUT SECRETS

If you are going to make some changes in the structure of your kitchen, here some layout tips the pros use, which you need to consider:

1. Entrances should be as wide as possible. It's hard to carry a lot of grocery bags through a small doorway.

2. Have at least one three-foot length of uninterrupted counter space for prepping meals.

3. Create counter space on each side of the sink, refrigerator, and stove for placing grocery bags and other cooking items.

4. Keep sharp edges to a minimum. Round out the corners of counters to eliminate bruises to you and the rest of your family.

5. The minimum width between an island and outer counter should be 42".

6. Allow for two feet of table or counter space per diner, with a one-foot deep opening for knee space.

7. Do not order your cabinetry until you pick out your appliances. Refrigerators and ovens come in different sizes, and you need to know your dimensions before you place your final order.

8. Consider the height of the cook! If you plan to use double-hung wall ovens, make sure you will be able to reach into the top oven without giving yourself third-degree burns.

9. Don't overlook vertical space, especially in a small kitchen. Hanging racks for pots can free up a much-needed cabinet for other things.

10. Design an eating area that meshes with your household's needs. Small children do better on counter-height barstools than bar-height ones. Or if you have enough room for a freestanding table, make sure you can walk all the way around it when it's time to set or clear the table.

PLAN YOUR OWN KITCHEN

Use a planning grid to help you figure out your new kitchen layout. This grid denotes a scale of ½" to 1'. Use a pencil (for brainstorming lots of changes!).

First, measure the length of your room and lay out the walls on the grid. Be sure to include doorways and windows. Next, write in anything that can't be moved or changed. Then create a template for each of the appropriate kitchen elements listed in the following table to scale. This will help you accurately plan a new layout. Lay down the pieces of your new kitchen. If you are too cramped when opening your

TABLE 1.1

Space Planner - Typical dimensions of cabinets and appliances.

ELEMENT	TYPICAL APPROXIMATE DIMENSIONS	OPTIONS
Doorways	36" W	Consider widening or moving.
Windows	36" W	Large windows expand the space.
Counter height	36" H × 24" D	Width varies with layout.
Aisles	42–48" W	Between countertops.
Base cabinet	9–48" W × 35" H × 24" D	Sink, single or double doors, stack of drawers, drawer/door combo.
Wall cabinet (large for dishes and glassware; small for spices)	12–48" W × 30–48" H × 12" D	Height depends on ceiling, size and type of molding used.
Pantry/utility cabinet (for food storage and large items)	9–48" W × 35" H × 12–24" D	Door front or sliding-out option. Deep cabinets require pullout extensions.
Built-in over-the-refrigerator cabinet	36" W × 18" H × 24" D	Measure refrigerator first. Trim kits fill in gaps.
Corner cabinet	36" W × 35" H × 46" D	Carousel used for multi-shelving and waste container storage options.
Trash cabinet	18–24" W × 35" H × 24 " D	Holds one or two bins next to or behind each other.
Dish rack cabinet	24–35" W × 12–15" H × 12" D	Slotted bottom to drip into sink, should span sink width.
Custom shelving	8–36" W × ¾" H × 12" D	Cut to fit sizing and styling, longer lengths may sag without bracing.
Small drawers	9–36" W × 3" H × 24" D	Custom inserts available.
Large drawers	9–36" W × 8–9" H × 24" D	Heavy glides for smoother operation.
Refrigerator, small	30–32" W × 68" H × 28–30" D	Plastic interiors, fewer options.
Refrigerator, large	32–48" W × 68–78" H × 30–36" D	Glass shelving, deep drawers, icemakers.
Dishwasher	24" W × 34" H	Rinse, china, and delay cycles, plain front, integrated panel.
Range	30–42" W × 36" H × 26" D	Gas, electric, or dual fuel with convection options.
Cooktop	30–48" W × 15–20" H × 24" D	Gas, electric, induction power; options with steamers, griddles, hot plates.
Single wall oven	26–36" W × 27–28" H × 24" D	Consider the interior dimensions.
Single/double wall oven /microwave available	24–30" W × 36–42" H × 24" D	Combination convection.
Ice maker	15–18" W × 35" H × 24" D	Pounds made per hour vary dramatically.
Wine cooler	15–24" W × 34¾" H × 24" D	Stainless steel shelving and variable climate control.

refrigerator, try placing it in a new spot on the grid. If a seldom-used desk area can be converted to a prep area, try switching things around. By playing with the floor plan, you'll get to know better what can and can't work depending upon the physical elements of the room (**1.7**).

Choosing the Style for Your Kitchen

Style and layout are two separate design functions. As you've seen, layout determines where things need to go to be efficient. Style results when you create a visual statement. Developing a style usually involves choosing specific shapes, colors, textures, and lighting. Style can either shout or whisper, depending on the elements you choose.

Defining your particular style can be difficult. Have you ever gone to someone's home and entered a room only to feel like you belong there? And then later, upon reflection, it's almost impossible to figure out why you actually liked the room. Was it the wall color or the furniture arrangement? It probably wasn't one thing over another but all the elements combined together! That's exactly what style is. And that's why there's a whole industry of professionals who make a living

▶ **1.7** Once you've created your grid and drawn in fixed elements, you can move appliances and furniture around.

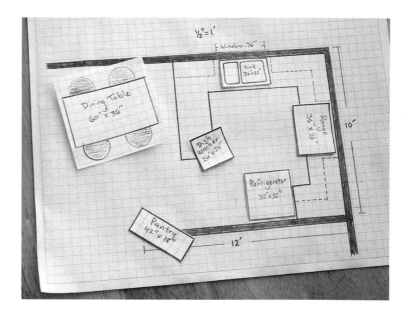

asking questions, listening to the answers, and creating rooms out of nothing. Interior designers, decorators, and architects make it seem easy. So let's steal some plays from their book.

STEP ONE: EXAMINE THE REST OF YOUR HOUSE

The best kitchens reflect the style that already exists in the rest of the house. If you want your kitchen to be dramatic, quirky, or strange, that's fine, just make sure it goes with the rest of your décor. Because of the sheer expense of designing a kitchen, you probably will not be changing its style again, so choose something you will not get tired of. And because it's one of the few rooms in the house everyone uses, your kitchen should be pleasing to everyone in the family, not just your own taste.

With style, continuity and flow can be achieved by using colors and materials that appear elsewhere in the house. So look around your house and see which rooms you like the best. What features do they have that you can incorporate into the kitchen? For example, when flooring options and/or wall color are unified throughout the house, especially in adjoining rooms, it makes a great statement and attests to your visual acuity and design prowess! Why not continue it into the kitchen?

■Don't Be Trendy!

Just like clothing, there are kitchen trends that change over time. It's easy to spot a kitchen from the 60's—avocado green appliances! The 70's—orange Formica countertops! The 80's—the all-white kitchen! The 90's—granite and stainless steel! And on and on it will go. The latest trends now include multi-height surfaces and commercial-grade appliances. But that doesn't mean you must have them in order to have a great kitchen. Don't be tempted to jump on the bandwagon of the latest trend, especially if it will kill your budget. It's important to make sure the installed elements of your kitchen are timeless and classic, and not so trendy that you become tired of them quickly.

STEP TWO: ESTABLISH A FOCAL POINT

A focal point is a spot where the eye is drawn naturally. A picture on the wall in a contrasting color can create a focal point. Or it could be a sleek oven hood that makes a statement with bold lines. It could be an interesting island made up of contrasting cabinets and colors from the rest of the kitchen. Make the focal point something that is unique to your kitchen. Be inspired: a piece of pottery, a small painting, or an antique sign all can be inspirations for creating the look of the kitchen (**1.8**). The focal point will determine the style for the rest of the kitchen.

▲ **1.8** A focal point draws the eye to a particular spot in your kitchen.

Be Realistic

Highly stylized kitchens can cost a ton of money. Much of the budget gets eaten by cabinetry or specialized storage components that help create a minimalist look. If that is the style you are drawn to, you may only be able to afford a room that achieves part of the look. If so, work with what you can afford, and be happy to move on.

The number of items you own and want in your kitchen can also help you determine the style that works for you. For example, it's hard to pull off minimalism while you're displaying your collection of antique menus plastered all over the walls.

STEP THREE: WORK WITH WHAT'S WORKED FOR OTHERS

Examine the following design styles. Focus on the various design elements and see which appeal to you. If you're a purist, you'll probably like most of the elements from one particular style. If you want to be creative, pick and choose elements that you like from many different themes. Then find some decorating magazines, see if you can spot each of these styles, and decide if you like how they work in kitchen settings.

In a practical sense, it's very difficult to keep within only one style. Combining different looks can really add to the unique style you call your own. However, in kitchens, the style is most usually differentiated by cabinetry choices.

Traditional: The use of fine woods, crown moldings, and darker colors evoke a sense of formality and refined taste (**1.9**). Current traditional kitchen trends include adding feet and legs to cabinets to mimic the look of furniture.

Country: The use of painted or beadboard cabinetry and rustic metals like iron and copper set the tone of a country kitchen.

Exposed bricks, salvaged beams, and recycled objects create a sense of connection with the past. Colors usually have a soft, worn look about them. Collectables, antique breadbaskets, vintage canisters, and simple floral and fruit motifs add to the look. There are several variations of "country," including French country (**1.10**), Early American cottage (**1.11**), and Shaker style (**1.12**). Current trends include retro appliances like the Aga ovens, distressed wood countertops, and large farmhouse sinks, which create an updated country style.

Contemporary: Simple flat-faced, linear cabinetry combined with sleek surfaces create the ultimate contemporary kitchen. Storage systems hide everyday tools to minimize clutter.

▼ **1.9** Many people feel comfortable with traditional kitchen décor.

▶ **1.10** A French country kitchen design.

▼ **1.11** Early-American cottage-style country kitchen.

Modern materials like stainless steel, glass tiles, and concrete are used frequently. Colors are usually cool in tone and muted. Black and white figures prominently, although a bold accent color can be a focal point (**1.13**). Lighting is recessed and lacking ornamentation. Current trends include industrial materials for cabinetry, unusual sinks/faucets mounted above countertops, and disappearing exhaust systems.

▲ **1.13** A contemporary style of kitchen provides a modern, cool look.

Eclectic: Eclectic kitchens are usually a continuum of an eclectic house. Elements are a mix of old and new; when combined they produce a look that reflects a highly-personalized style (**1.14**). This look is ideal if you are working on a budget, or using refurbished cabinets and recycled flooring. Items collected from travels and hand-me-down accessories complete the look.

STEP FOUR: SHOPPING FOR THE RIGHT ELEMENTS

Once you've figured out what design elements you want to keep in your kitchen, and what you are absolutely dying to get rid of, there is probably an in-between group of things that you're not sure about. Now is the time to make some decisions. By spending your money on quality cabinets, countertops, fixtures, and appliances, you'll be sure to enjoy them for years to come. If your budget doesn't allow for top-of-the-line items, use the following guide to learn about the pros and cons of various choices. Rest assured that with proper selection, installation, and care, you will have a beautiful kitchen.

▼ **1.14** An eclectic style might be just for you.

▲ 1.15 Framed cabinets are the most common type these days.

Cabinets

All stock, semi-custom, or custom cabinets are constructed with plywood, particle board, or medium density fiberboard (MDF). As with anything, quality varies with the material used. Cabinets can be constructed in one of two ways: framed or frameless. Framed cabinets have a 1"–1½" frame installed on the front of the box. This allows the door to be attached as either a full or partial overlay, meaning that the hinges on the doors show and that the doors don't necessarily meet each other (**1.15**). Frameless cabinets, also known as Eurostyle, have no front frame so the interior is completely accessible. The door can only be attached as a full overlay with a concealed hinge (**1.16**).

Popular exterior finishes are solid wood, wood veneers, laminate, melamine (low density laminate), or Thermafoil.

▼ 1.16 Frameless cabinets are also called Eurostyle—they give a modern feel.

Solid wood can be finished in many different ways that transform its look: one type of wood can literally be changed to look like another. Paint, stain, and glaze can be further altered by their finish: crackle, sanded, or distressed. Wood veneer and laminate don't have the same problems of cracking or warping as regular wood, and they are considerably less expensive than solid wood. Wood veneer is actually a thin slice of wood attached to a substrate, usually medium density particle board (MDF). Laminate is similar to wood veneer in that its surface is a thin composite of plastic and resin fused together under high pressure attached to a substrate. Even though laminate and wood veneer can suffer damage by chipping and separating seams, with proper care they can be beautiful and last a lifetime. With so many design choices and their reasonable cost, they should be considered if solid wood isn't affordable. Thermafoil is made from sheets of polyvinyl chloride. They are melted, molded, and shaped around MDF. As the least expensive option, Thermafoil may or may not hold up under your kitchen's particular environment. It's prone to bubbling and peeling when exposed to heat, and can yellow with exposure to the sun. I guess that explains why it's so popular in basements!

The cabinet's facing is often different than the materials used in its interior, which can include melamine, wood veneer, plywood, or laminate. It's best to get an interior that is easy to keep clean, so ask about the options when ordering new cabinetry.

Compartments with drawers are constructed in a variety of ways. The ones with interlocked corners, known as dovetailed, are better than those that are glued together (**1.17**). The drawer glides should open smoothly and self-close. The glides can be side mounted, under-mounted, or integrated. Under-mounted slides with roller channel glides are the best option because the mechanics are completely hidden and don't compromise the size of the drawers. Better cabinets offer drawers with a full extension; this allows complete access to the back of the drawer (**1.18**).

Hinge options abound including concealed, overlay, wrap-around, flush-mount, and decorative. Make sure that you examine how wide the hinge allows the cabinet door to open.

▲ **1.17** A well-constructed drawer uses dovetail joints.

▲ **1.18** Under-mounted drawer glides with full extension provide access to the back of the drawer.

If you want your hinges to show, make sure they are attractive and complement the cabinetry.

Hardware

Doorknobs and drawer pulls contribute toward delineating the style of a kitchen. They are an effective finishing touch that can really pull a room together, especially if you are following an eclectic style. When choosing new hardware, it's best to try out a few different choices and see how they fit into your style scheme. Consider letting all family members examine them and make sure they are a good fit for everyone's hands. However, don't install any until you choose: once you've made holes in the cabinetry, you're stuck with limiting your options to something that will match the holes. For example, drawer pulls can come as knobs or handles: handles require two holes while knobs require only one.

Countertops

Beautiful countertops are high on the list of potential renovations for most homeowners. Countertops can either make a statement or fade into the background, depending on what you have chosen as your focal point. Countertops should be durable, water-resistant, and easy to keep clean. They must put up with spills, stains, clutter, fingerprints, pen marks and all the accidents of everyday living.

A new kitchen trend is to install countertops at varying heights to accommodate different tasks. For example, you might want a higher countertop for cutting and chopping, and a lower one for kneading dough. This design would break up a long work surface, which may be more appealing. Island countertops can be the same material or different from the outlying counters (**1.19**). A raised counter acts as a natural buffer from the cook zone, but an island with one height can also double as a large buffet area.

Countertops are now made of some of the most durable materials, both natural and man-made. Here is a list of the most popular choices. Read carefully and choose the best one for your family's lifestyle: each comes with distinctive pros and cons.

▲ **1.19** This quartz island countertop contrasts nicely with solid-color countertops in the rest of the kitchen.

Granite, marble, limestone: Natural stone is popular because it's beautiful, unique, and almost impossible to damage. Hot pots can be placed directly on it, and water glasses will never leave a ring (**1.20**). However, all natural stones are somewhat porous and can stain, especially with substances like red wine

▲ **1.20** Natural stone countertops are beautiful and difficult to damage.

or cooking oils. Natural stones vary in their hardness as well as their color. Marble and limestone are the most porous, but if properly treated can last for years. Granite is the hardest of the stones and the most durable over time.

Natural stones are sold in slabs, and need to be custom cut to fit your countertops. When shopping, choose a reputable stone dealer that will let you pick a slab from their stone yard, or choose a stone dealer that will guarantee the integrity of the slab. Because most stone is shipped from overseas, there is a limit to the size of the slab. If your countertop is longer than a slab, you will need to match two pieces of stone (another reason to be there to pick it out), which will be installed next to each other with a seam. The seam is often quite noticeable and unattractive. To avoid this seam, many kitchen designers will carefully lay out where the appliances fall within the countertop, or mix two different countertop materials, such as natural stone and natural wood.

Another drawback of natural stone is the price. It is the most expensive countertop option. You'll pay for every cutout, and all but the most basic edges cost extra. Natural stone must be sealed yearly, which calls for an additional expense if you choose not to do it yourself. Lastly, because stone is so hard, anything fragile you drop on it will break. I've lost many glasses this way!

Manufactured quartz: Another high-end countertop option is man-made "stone," called manufactured quartz. This material is virtually indestructible. Quartz is almost as hard as diamond, practically impossible to scratch, and non-porous so it doesn't need to be sealed. Unlike granite, where each piece is unique, there is uniformity to the surface patterns. Unfortunately, it's still very expensive and can actually be more expensive for smaller kitchens because there are minimum costs associated for the manufacturer that bump up the cost per square foot. There are a limited number of colors available, although the manufacturers are creating more each year (**1.21**).

Solid surfaces: Solid surface refers to a man-made combination of acrylic and polyester that has color blended within. Often called by their individual brand names such as Swanstone, Corian, or Avonite, these materials are completely man-made. The entire countertop—including the sink—can be made of the same material, often in one continuous piece, in either the same or different colors (**1.22**). Solid surfaces are advantageous because the color choice is almost unlimited, and if you have a

▼ **1.21** Manufactured quartz is almost as hard as diamond.

DESIGNING YOUR SPACE

very large kitchen, the color of the countertop will always be uniform. These come in a wide variety of designs, from a solid color to a duplicate of natural stone. Unfortunately, they can be very expensive, and prone to scratches, stains, and susceptible to heat. Small repairs can be made, though, and many homeowners love these sold-surface countertops.

▼ **1.22** Solid-surface countertops can be made in a variety of colors and as one continuous piece.

Concrete: Concrete countertops are very trendy, and because they are custom-made, they can come in a wide variety of colors. The concrete is actually poured and molded to fit your kitchen design so that you don't have the seams that you would with natural stone (**1.23**). Note that concrete can be cold, rough, and expensive. And, once this trend has cooled, it might be something that goes out of date.

▼ **1.23** Concrete is poured and molded to your kitchen design.

Wood: Wood options, including butcher block, have long been associated with casual or country kitchens. Plank hardwood countertops are making a comeback in high-end kitchens today. Wood is warm to the touch and evokes a sense of comfort (**1.24**). Exotic woods can cost more than some solid surfaces but have a unique, luxurious feel about them. Most manufacturers seal the wood with either oil or polyurethane, both of which need to be redone periodically. Wood can warp, crack, and mar badly, but that can add to its uniqueness. Some homeowners request that the countertop be "distressed" before installation so they won't have to worry about nicks and stains after that.

▼ **1.24** Wood counters add a warm homey feel to your kitchen.

Stainless steel: Commercial kitchens use stainless steel because they are the easiest to clean, and restaurants need to maintain strict health standards (**1.25**). Stainless steel is durable, completely non-absorbent, and a perfect choice for a sleek, modern style kitchen. However, these countertops are very expensive to install. Worse, if you are a true neat freak, you'll be disappointed when every little water mark and fingerprint shows.

▼ **1.25** Stainless steel is a good choice for a modern-looking kitchen.

Tile: Tile can be arranged and patterned in a million different ways, creating a countertop that makes a design statement truly unique to your home (**1.26**). Tile is water-resistant and heat proof. The cost can range from reasonable to expensive, depending on the price of the tile. Relatively fragile, tile chips easily when things are dropped on it, and it is difficult to replace a single tile, or even a small group of tiles. Hence, more and more, tile is being relegated for the backsplash (the part of the wall directly behind the countertop). Cleaning stained grout lines is the number one gripe of tile countertops, followed by the uneven surface it ultimate creates. If tile is your number one choice, choose a dark tile and grout color.

▼ 1.26 It's best to choose a dark color for kitchen countertop tile.

Laminate: Laminate is the best choice when cost is a factor. Laminates, often known by their individual brand names such as Formica or Wilsonart, are durable, water-resistant, and easy to clean. They are made from a process that combines chemistry and photography, by attaching plastic veneer to particleboard. Laminates are offered in a wide range of available colors, textures, and patterns (**1.27**). However, don't be too quick to pick one that mimics stone or marble. It may look great on that small chip, but when used to cover a large area, it really isn't effective aesthetically. A better choice would be to choose a laminate that wants to be a laminate.

The drawbacks to laminates are that they are not indestructible. Lighter colors stain easily. The edges of the counter are prone to chip and can't be repaired easily; also, they often stain and become very dark and noticeable.

▶ **1.27** Laminates can mimic other materials, such as wood, but they are not indestructible.

A wood trim can help protect the edges, but the dark seams are unavoidable. Also, because laminates are not particularly heavy, you must use drop-in sinks, which create more dirty seams and are difficult to maintain.

Plumbing Fixtures

Something as utilitarian as the kitchen sink can be a focal point of a well-functioning kitchen. And the right one is really a matter of preference. Some cooks swear by a single deep basin. If you want to hide a drying rack, you might want to consider two basins. Most sinks are 7–9" deep, but deeper ones can be special-ordered.

Popular sink materials are stainless steel, porcelain, enamel-covered steel, solid surface, stone, or copper (**1.28**). The type of countertop dictates the choice of under-mount or drop-in

◀ **1.28** Stainless steel is a common kitchen sink material.

installation. An under-mount sink means that its rim doesn't show above the counter (**1.29**). This eliminates unsightly caulking, which looks even worse when it eventually stains. If you are choosing a laminate countertop, you are restricted to a drop-in sink, which sits on top of the counter (**1.30**).

Faucets can be another important element in the kitchen. They are an inexpensive way to upgrade your kitchen and provide an entirely different look. There are now designer faucets that have built in sprayers, hoses, and water filters. Choose a faucet that enhances the style of your kitchen. A simple linear one-handled faucet might look great in a modern kitchen, where a farmhouse-style faucet suits a more traditional type of kitchen (**1.31**).

Before you pick out a faucet, make sure your tallest pot can fit inside the sink and under the faucet. Also, if you have small children, a single handle that pre-mixes hot water with cold can help prevent accidental burns.

▶ **1.29** An under-mount sink avoids the need to caulk around the rim.

▲ 1.31 Choose a faucet style that fits with your kitchen décor.

▲ 1.30 Drop-in sinks sit on top of the counter.

Flooring

Flooring is an often-overlooked element in the design scheme. In a well-appointed kitchen, there are a few rules that must be carefully considered regarding flooring. Dark colors will draw the eye downward, and every little scratch shows. Lighter colors are harder to keep clean. Patterns and textures shouldn't compete with other focal points in the room.

The best kitchen flooring choice will be one that flows with the existing flooring from the rest of the house in either color or style. The following are the most up-to-date options available. Many of the options for countertop materials are also available for flooring, and their benefits and drawbacks will be similar as well.

■Wall-to-Wall Coverage

If you are completely gutting the kitchen, make sure the new flooring is installed "wall to wall," before the cabinets are put in. This will offer more flexibility in the future, in case you need to replace your appliances. The added tile will change the final floor-to-ceiling measurement, shortening it an inch or so. This could affect the size of the backsplash or change the placement of the upper cabinets.

Natural stone (granite, marble, slate, sandstone, limestone): Stone tiles are usually the most expensive tiles you can buy (**1.32**). With proper care, they will last forever. They can be made waterproof by sealing, but the finish should be honed or dulled, rather than polished, in order to make them less slippery when wet. Depending on the grade purchased, they may have to be filled to account for hollow pockets.

▶ **1.32** Natural stone tile, like this marble floor, can be costly, but it is beautiful and lasts forever.

However, there are drawbacks. The acoustics and comfort level should be addressed. Sound will bounce directly off stone floors, and when mixed with stone countertops and vaulted ceilings, even the quietest conversation can become deafening. Stone floors are not very malleable, so standing on them for some time while cooking might be uncomfortable on the back and feet for some.

Tile (clay, porcelain): Porcelain tile is a better floor choice than ceramic as long as the color runs through the tile, instead of being glazed onto the surface. Then, if the tile chips, it will be less noticeable. The endless availability of color combinations and patterns can seem overwhelming. A good design strategy is to stick with one light color that you can live with and add some darker accents. Like stone, some people find standing on tile tiring (**1.33**).

▼ **1.33** Clay tile is attractive, but because it is uniform, chips will be noticed. It can also be uncomfortable to stand on.

Concrete: Concrete flooring, long the staple of coffee houses, retail shops, and restaurants, has found a market in home kitchens. Interesting new colors are available and can give a kitchen instant hip style (**1.34**). Concrete needs to be sealed like stone. If you want to see how a concrete floor will wear, look no further than your garage. On the down side, concrete is cold, slightly rough, and hard. Worse, just forget about anything that drops on it!

▼ **1.34** Concrete floors can give your kitchen a unique style.

Wood: Hardwood floors are a good choice for both period and modern styles (**1.35**). Wood is more forgiving than stone or tile, but less durable. It can be scratched by moving chairs or appliances. Small scratches can be "colored" to be less noticeable. If necessary, the whole floor can be painted or refinished without being completely replaced.

Pre-refinished veneer flooring is not recommended for the kitchen. Too many small gaps occur when being installed, making it unsanitary. For hardwood, make sure to quickly wipe up any water spills: they can damage the floor. Small throw rugs can protect prep and sink areas from too much wear and tear. Frequent vacuuming (rather than sweeping) can lengthen the life of the floor immeasurably.

▼ **1.35** Hardwood floors enhance just about any kitchen décor, including this country motif.

Vinyl: Vinyl was once the hope of all mankind. Its reasonable price and claims of easy cleaning and maintenance swayed many. But in a kitchen with heavy traffic, vinyl flooring can't take the heat. Prone to discoloring a dingy yellow, it dents when things are dropped on it. It tears and seams split when water gets under it. However, its softness and pliability make it the easiest option for serious cooks who are constantly on their feet.

All vinyl flooring is man-made and comes in a wide variety of colors, designs, and textures. It can be made in one continuous sheet or in individual tiles. The inexpensive production technique of rotogravure fuses vinyl layers together with a protective top. The more expensive inlaid variety fuses vinyl crystals together with a protective top. Once you wear through the top of either, you'll never regain the look it had when it was brand new.

Commercial vinyl tiles: An alternative to sheet vinyl are vinyl tiles, which wear better because their color is continuous through the tile. Commercial tiles come in a huge array of colors and patterns. Unfortunately, they get dull and dirty with wear and need to be sealed and buffed. Have you ever seen one of those big buffing machines in a neighbor's house? That is why they are more often used in commercial applications.

Linoleum: Linoleum has some of the same issues as vinyl flooring, but wears better and is easier to maintain. It's soft under foot, easy to install, and relatively inexpensive. Old linoleum was made with asbestos, so think twice about trying to take up an old floor yourself: call an expert. New linoleum is considered a better environmental choice because it is made from natural linseed oil, wood pulp, rosin, and pigment powder (**1.36**). Unfortunately, linoleum needs to be either sealed or polished. Like wood, solvents and water don't mix with linoleum flooring.

Cork: Cork flooring is a natural beautiful product made from the bark of a tree, so it is the "greenest" floor around. Cork is not recommended for the kitchen, however. Water is cork's worst enemy and the floor is so soft it will dent with heavy traffic use. Even though cork flooring can be sealed, it just won't hold up in the kitchen.

◀ 1.36 Modern linoleum wears well and is easy to maintain.

Lighting

Unfortunately, lighting is usually overlooked by most people. Aside from replacing a bulb with a brighter wattage, most people just go about their business, squinting while they work. But the right amounts of light in a kitchen can really make a significant difference. A great kitchen needs a combination of natural, ambient, task, decorative, and accent lighting. Before you assess your lighting needs, the layout and design of the work areas must already be established.

First assess how much natural light the kitchen gets. Too much light from a window can be regulated by an adjustable window treatment. Don't forget to remain within the style of the kitchen, and pick something that matches your selected style in color and texture.

Second, analyze the ambient light. Ambient light contributes to the mood of a room. That's why low-lit restaurants appear more intimate than brightly-light diners. If you only

▲ **1.37** Under-cabinet lighting, like these xenon strips, will help brighten up your workspace.

change one thing in your kitchen, it should be to put dimmers on all the lights. It's a great option to be able to adjust the lights down low when you are making coffee in the morning or sneaking a midnight snack!

Next, examine the work areas and see if there is enough task lighting. Task lighting can be mounted on the ceiling or underneath a cabinet to brighten up counter space (**1.37**). If you choose track lighting, make sure to install it so that you don't create shadows where you will be standing. If you install under-cabinet lighting, hidden electric socket strips are great to hide the plugs. Also, consider installing a thin-style trim, called light rail, to hide the fixtures further from view.

Don't forget about decorative and accent lights. Two great places for inspiration are over the sink and the island. Perhaps you can exchange an old ceiling fan for a chandelier. Even a small funky desk lamp in the corner can add visual interest to the kitchen.

■A Word About Light Bulbs

Usually, incandescent, fluorescent, and halogen lamps are combined to make just the right lighting plan. Incandescent bulbs are what most people use in their homes for ambient and task lighting. They are a warmer, yellower light. Incandescent bulbs can now be found "color corrected"—those bulbs are blue and produce a whiter, clearer light. Fluorescent bulbs are typically found in offices, garages, or workrooms. They use less energy than incandescent, but are much brighter. Most people don't care for the harshness that fluorescent bulbs emit over an entire room, but they are very effective for task lighting. Halogen lights are a whiter, cooler version of incandescent light that run on much less energy. Unfortunately, they emit so much heat that they can literally give you a third degree burn when touched. New technology is producing better fluorescent and halogen bulbs that address some of these issues. Newer fluorescents aren't as harsh nor do they flicker as badly. Newer halogen types don't emit as much heat, but they aren't as bright either. Halogens can be used for ambient, task, or accent lighting.

Choosing Appliances

Choosing appliances *for the kitchen is like a chess game. You must try to figure out your moves ahead of time so you can anticipate what you'll be doing later. This is especially true if you are not purchasing all of the appliances at the same time. The big three—refrigerator, stove, and dishwasher— dominate the kitchen landscape. Their exterior design is important from an aesthetic point of view, but in reality what kind of cook you are and how your household operates should dictate your choices.*

The Good Ole Icebox

Refrigerators seem to rank with SAT scores: it doesn't matter how great yours is, someone's is always better. Manufacturers are capitalizing on our insatiable need for bigger, better, and best. Refrigerators today can range from $500 to $10,000, with most falling between $800-$3000. Knowing the options available will help you decide what your family, and your kitchen, really requires.

Choosing a refrigerator should be all about food storage—how many people need to be fed. Capacity is measured in cubic feet, and the average is 4-5 cubic feet per person. Try to allow 24 cubic feet for a family of four. If your fridge is too small, you'll be spending too much time rearranging the contents whenever you need to find something. And if you are a bulk shopper, you'll need plenty of space for oversized packages.

Next, determine what style of refrigerator you want. This really depends on how much bending you want to do. Do you want to bend over for the frozen food or for the fresh food? The three basic configurations are top mount, bottom mount, and side-by-side (referring to where the freezer is located).

If you want ice cream to stare directly back at you with a loving gaze, choose a top mount, which has the freezer over the refrigerator. Here you'll find the ice maker and frozen foods easily accessible at eye level. The refrigerator compartment of a top mount typically holds the most fresh food. Also, large casseroles, cakes, and platters can be easily stored on the wide shelving (**2.1**).

Bottom-mount models have the refrigerator compartment on top with the freezer below (**2.2**). If you rarely eat frozen food, you won't mind bending for stuff in the freezer. The bottom compartment will hold your icemaker as well. If you want an ice maker in the door, you've got to go with either a top-mount or side-by-side model.

For some, the side-by-side refrigerator has the best of both worlds (**2.3**). You can set up your food so that you access items you use most from both the freezer and refrigerator at eye level. The freezers usually have at least one pullout bin for large items. Just make sure the freezer can hold your favorite frozen pizza boxes.

▲ **2.1** Top-mount refrigerators typically provide the most space for fresh food.

▲ **2.2** Bottom-mount refrigerators put the freezer on the bottom.

▶ **2.3** Side-by-side refrigerators may be the most convenient.

The most expensive models often combine these elements. I've seen refrigerators that look like side-by-sides with a bottom freezer drawer. This works if you do lots of cooking ahead of time and freeze your meals. There are also refrigerated drawers that work alongside the traditional unit to offer easy access for beverages, as well as additional space.

INTERIOR OPTIONS

Next, consider what kind of shelving appeals to you. The choices are either glass or wire. Glass is easy to clean and looks posh. The shelving should be adjustable so you can personalize your refrigerator space. There are lots of other nifty options you can purchase but they may be a waste of money. Does anyone use that egg container? Do you really need a compartment that defrosts meat, or keeps cheese at the exact right temperature? Bins that are temperature-adjustable and can keep veggies fresh are a popular choice. But does it work for your family?

THE ICE MAKER: FRIEND OR FOE?

Ice makers are the number one service call for all refrigerator problems. Yet they are pretty standard equipment for most high-end refrigerators. Ice can be dispensed from the door, but that will eat up your freezer space. Water filtering systems have gotten pretty sophisticated so the taste is consistent with bottled water. Inquire about the water filter system used and the cost of replacement filters. Last, make sure you have the salesperson turn on the refrigerator and the ice maker so you can hear how noisy they are.

Efficiency Counts!

Choose an appliance with an Energy Star rating. Compare the yellow tag of your favorite choices and see which one will save you money in the long haul. A typical refrigerator will last for at least a decade, and energy prices are only going to go up. Although side-by-side refrigerator/freezers use somewhat more electricity than an over/under style, they offer the most capacity and convenience.

The Dishwasher

The dishwasher is the workhorse of the kitchen, your faithful and intrepid assistant. Dishwashers come in many shapes and sizes so there is a lot of information to consider before buying one. If you allow the dishwasher to do what it's capable of doing, you can save yourself tons of time. Dishwashers use water pressure to clean the dishes; the force of the water coming from the spraying arm actually does the cleaning. Each rack should have its own cleaning arm, sometimes they have more. Get a dishwasher that has at least two cleaning arms.

Remember how you used to just about clean your dishes before putting them into the dishwasher? The best feature to be developed is the "rinse only" cycle. If your dishwasher has this, you are in business. Aside from scraping off the largest food particles, bones, seeds, and pits, you just place your dishes in the machine and hit "rinse only." The addition of a garbage disposal at the bottom of the dishwasher virtually eliminates worrying about pieces of food clogging the drain. When timing is an issue, you'll love the fact that you can throw your big pots and bowls in for a rinse while you're still cooking and not take up all the space in your sink.

Some dishwashers claim to scrub your pots for you. High heat coils similar to ones used to clean your oven actually bake off the crusts from your pots and pans. Talk about saving a manicure! This can be hit or miss depending upon just how dirty your pots are. You might have to run them through a second time to get them completely clean.

New integrated designs mean that your dishwasher's controls are positioned on the top of the door and only visible when you open it. This has its pluses and minuses. On the plus side, the front of the door can be a beautiful stainless steel panel or made to match your cabinetry. On the down side, you have to open the door to make any changes in the cycle.

Also available are the new dishwasher drawers. These seem like a great idea. Two separate dishwashers that can work together or independently fit in the 24" space of a conventional dishwasher. Or, if you are doing a bit of remodeling, you can place one on each side of your sink. Drawers can help eliminate the bending involved in loading and unloading.

INTERIOR CONFIGURATIONS

From coffee cups to champagne flutes, everything needs to fit inside without breaking. No one wants to be hand washing crystal anymore—who has the time? After a fabulous dinner party, you want to be able to easily load all your stemware on the top rack, so adjustable racks in your dishwasher are essential. Before you go to the store, measure the tallest glass you own and take the measurements with you. There is nothing worse than not being able to load your dishwasher with the glasses you already have.

IMPORTANT EXTRA FEATURES

All dishwashers manufactured today use less water than those made even five years ago. Once again, check for the Energy Star rating. A dishwasher's noise level, or lack thereof, is also a huge selling point. If your kitchen is part of a great room, the amount of noise your appliances make can be a real problem. Many kitchens are now designed as "open kitchens," which are part of or adjacent to other rooms. These areas tend to be family rooms or dens where people watch television, read, or play video games. The noise of the dishwasher can really be annoying if it's reverberating loudly throughout the space and competing with your surround sound audio system. If you have a kitchen that doesn't connect with other rooms, noise level won't matter as much.

Programmable cleaning cycles abound in dishwasher land. You really only need the normal, rinse only, energy saver, and time delay cycles. Normal is used most frequently when the machine is completely filled and ready to run after dinner. Rinse is great for breakfast dishes that sit until nighttime, or while you are cooking and want to throw your pots in before they get crusty. Energy saver usually lets dishes air-dry instead of using the heat elements. In theory it's a great idea, but water won't completely evaporate from your plasticware and then you have to air-dry it on the counter anyway. The time-delay function helps when you want to load up the dishwasher after dinner and let it rip after you've gone to bed.

Cooktops

Cooking at home is supposed to be easy, but with the choices available today it has never been more complicated. The variety in cooking surfaces, speeds, and energy sources for cooking has greatly increased. In order to make the right decision for you and your family, first sit down with your project log and jot down a few things about yourself: What do you like to cook? How much time do you have to cook? How many people are you cooking for? Aside from these questions, your choice will be dictated by your cooking needs, your décor, and last but not least, your pocketbook.

Back in the old days, oh, say, twenty years ago, people who entertained regularly needed lots of equipment to cook a lot of food. Most people invested in a separate cooktop as well as dual wall ovens. This allowed them to prepare large quantities of food simultaneously. Fortunately, new technologies have made vast improvements that enhance existing appliances to shorten cooking time. Now appliances can often perform more than one task, saving space and money.

Generally speaking, your choice of cooking surfaces will be dictated by the type of home energy source you have. If your home is accessible to a gas line, your options abound. If not, you will have to stick to electrically run appliances. Here is the lowdown on each of the options.

Gas cooktops: Die-hard chefs and Foodies will tell you that cooking with gas far surpasses electricity. First of all, gas burners heat instantly. You can eyeball the flame quickly to the heat you want. There's practically no waiting time for pans to heat up. What chefs really love about gas is temperature correction. If you need to lower the temperature, you can do so instantaneously. There is usually one burner that heats faster and quicker than others because it outputs a higher amount of BTUs (British Thermal Unit), a unit of heat energy. The more BTUs, the higher the heat output. For example, the higher the BTUs, the faster your water will boil. Many cooktops have a combination of small, medium, and large burners. In addition to various sized burners, high-end manufacturers have added options like griddle pans, grills, and wok burners to further

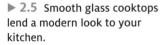

▲ **2.4** High-end gas stoves include options to make the gas cooktop more versatile than ever.

enhance a cooktop's performance (**2.4**). An important feature to look for is a continuous grate that makes it easy to slide pans off one burner onto another.

On the down side, you can't turn on a gas burner and start doing something else. By the time you've answered the phone, for example, chances are you've burned your butter. So multi-tasking is out when using a gas stove.

Electric cooktops: These cooktops come with a huge variety of surfaces and different benefits. Most people are familiar with electric coil cooktops; these are pretty much the dinosaurs of cooking equipment and are rapidly being upstaged by a list that includes ceramic glass over the heat coils, magnetic induction surfaces, and solid cast burners. Coil burners can be had for very little money compared with the newer technologies. There's not much great to say about coil burners either. There is a delay in heating electric coils and once hot, they take longer for the temperature to be adjusted up or down. Traditional electric cooktops have coils and drip pans that protect the mechanics as well as reflect heat back to the cooking surface. They can be very hard to clean if your pots overflow. It's better to consider buying a cooktop that has sealed burners.

Other electric cooktop choices are solid-element or porcelain glass cooktops. The streamlined look of the smooth

▶ **2.5** Smooth glass cooktops lend a modern look to your kitchen.

glass top is very appealing to the eye (**2.5**). There are no unsightly burners to worry about; however, you need to be diligent about cleaning spills immediately. These burners will stay hot for a longer time than traditional electric coils, and there is an indicator light that glows as long as they are hot to the touch. They're easy to clean, but you have to be careful not to get burned by the steam if you need to wipe up a spill while it's still warm. The latest technology introduced and by far the most superior is the new halogen burner. With the speed of gas, halogen instantly heats and cools quickly.

Most porcelain cooktops are enamel coated and can be scratched easily. You have to be careful not to drag your pot once it's placed on the surface; instead, always lift it off. Also, certain types of aluminum and other metals can leave stains. If you wait too long, spills can be very difficult to scrub off and you're limited to soft sponges and non-abrasive cleansers. Solid element cooktops are slow to heat up but they hold their heat well, so they are great for a slow simmer.

Induction cooktops: This latest technology is a whole different animal. Induction cooking works by placing a magnetic pan onto a surface that has magnetic coils imbedded into it. When the pan connects with the surface, a current is created, which causes the pan to heat. Obviously, you need to have, or buy, magnetic pans. You can check your cookware by placing a magnet on the bottom. If the magnet sticks, the pan will work on this type of cooktop. Like gas, the temperatures can be controlled more efficiently than electric, and some even come with halogen burners. By the way, induction is the most energy-efficient means of cooking.

Ovens

Conventional ovens are powered by either gas or electricity, but be prepared to pay a lot more for the latter. Consensus is that electric ovens are better for baking. If you do a lot of entertaining you may want to invest in a double oven. Ovens can either be wall-mounted or come with the cooktop as a single unit, called a freestanding range. The interior space of a single unit is larger than a wall unit. Last, the self-cleaning feature is something to consider. While it works well, you need to remember that you can't ever use oven cleaners once you've committed to self-cleaning.

Convection ovens: If you are bored with conventional cooking, you must consider adding to or replacing your conventional oven with a convection oven—they are well worth the extra cost! Convection cooking works when air heated by an electric unit is blown around the food. Consequently, food cooks more evenly and faster, sometimes by as much as 50 percent. You can also load up your oven racks without worrying that some dishes will be overdone and some underdone: the air will maintain a more even cooking temperature throughout the oven. Convection ovens shine for baking pastries or roasts because the hot air gives the exterior of the food an excellent crust (**2.6**). You may have to spend a little time converting recipe cook times, although lots of new ovens do the math for you with onboard computer pads. However, the convection fan takes up space, leaving you with a smaller cooking space inside the oven.

▶ **2.6** The hot air of convection ovens is great for roasting food and baking pastries.

◀ **2.7** Freestanding ranges can combine both gas and electric cooking technologies.

Freestanding ranges: Freestanding ranges can have it all. Some feature dual fuel options, allowing for both gas heat and electric convection cooking (**2.7**). Others have small warming ovens or even microwaves built into what used to be the standard bottom utility drawers.

Commercial-grade appliances: Many homeowners are opting for cooktops and ovens that have features previously found only in commercial kitchens. If money is no object, you can buy professional series appliances that manufacturers make specifically for the home kitchen. These can include neat features such as steamers or deep fat fryers. Just remember that most professional series ovens are larger than the standard 30" and can throw off lots of heat, so your room has to be well ventilated.

Ventilation: Don't mistake an exhaust fan for an exhaust vent. An exhaust fan will clear the air of cooking odors, while an exhaust hood or vent will actually expel smoke and cooking odors from your home. Some cooktops have downdraft vents, which don't work quite as well as an overhead hood. A hood can be a focal point in your kitchen, although that may make it more expensive (**2.8**). Also, some microwave ovens come with a venting feature and can be placed over a cooktop for maximum efficiency.

▶ **2.8** A stylish exhaust hood can be a focal point of your kitchen.

Microwave Ovens

Few of us can live without a microwave. In fact, you can actually do most of your cooking with just a microwave and a toaster oven while you are under construction! As with all other appliances, microwave ovens have come a long way in a short amount of time. What sets individual microwave ovens apart is how powerful they are. The cheaper ones have less power, but they may be adequate if you don't use your microwave often. Because microwave ovens work on electricity, they are rated by their wattage, and 800 watts is the minimum you really want. Look for models with a turntable, which helps cook food more evenly. If you rely on a microwave for defrosting meats, look for a model that can ask for the weight and calculate the necessary minutes. Some microwaves offer convection oven systems, or use halogen light to drastically reduce cook times. These models can be expensive but are worth the money in the long run.

Must-Have Small Appliances

Small appliances are a necessary evil. On the one hand, they can really make your life easier so it's often impossible to think about living without them. And on the other hand, it's a chore to figure out how to store them all!

Small appliances complete the kitchen, which in turn completes the cook. The choices are endless when it comes to stuffing your house with gadgets. Therefore it's smart to sit down and figure out what you really think you'll use. No doubt the list is going to be a bit different for everyone. But there are definite must-have appliances that every well-stocked kitchen should include.

Finding the right one for you involves examining the various features each brand offers. For example, if you whip up smoothies every afternoon, make sure your blender is a master ice crusher and has a great warranty on the motor. What follows are the most common small appliances, and their features to consider.

MAKING COFFEE

The standards have been raised for home brewing. To feed our addiction, coffeemakers come in many shapes and sizes. Each

A Perfect Fit

If you are replacing an existing appliance, don't forget to measure the old appliance or the actual space it will be occupying. Buying the wrong size appliance can really turn into a headache. Also bring your tape measure to the store. Don't rely on a salesperson to give you correct information. Ask to see the specs and double-check the appliance yourself.

type has its own unique flavor, and as expected, its benefits and drawbacks.

Electric auto-drip machines are probably the most convenient way to make coffee. Just fill up the reservoir with cold water, add the right amount of ground coffee, and hit the On button. Insulated carafes now make it possible to keep coffee fresh for hours and eliminate the burnt smell of leftover coffee crusting to the bottom of the pot. Surprisingly, you can control the bitterness and overall flavor by using different filters. Paper filters produce a smoother cup, while reusable gold filters allow more flavor to emerge. Larger grinds are best with an auto-drip. The longer the water sits on the grinds, the more bitter the coffee will taste.

Old-fashioned **percolators** are now sold with programmable features like those found on auto-drip models. Percolators bubble water over the grinds, creating piping hot coffee that stays hot for hours. Cleaning is simple: you actually rinse the whole inside. The oily residue can be removed by perking a brew of water and white vinegar. Cleaning the basket that contains the grinds is harder than just throwing away the grinds in the paper filters of an auto-drip.

The **French press** is a beautiful piece of equipment, but brewing a good cup of coffee this way requires several steps. First, you have to boil the water. Then, after pouring it over the grinds, plunge down the grinds and wait for them to steep, up to five minutes or longer if you want strong coffee. This method is best for making 1–2 cups. If there is anything left over, it gets cold quickly and must be reheated in the microwave. Try an insulated French press coffeemaker in stainless that keeps the coffee warmer longer (**2.9**).

Espresso machines can be a fun addition to your coffee arsenal. Imagine whipping up the perfect cappuccino whenever you want one. Espresso machines vary in price from $50 to $5000 for a built-in gold-plated device. What you really need to keep in mind is how efficiently the machine heats water. There should be a valve that allows you to adjust the flow rate so that you can slow it down for hotter espresso. Also, espresso machines are judged by how well they make steam. A good machine can build up a lot of pressure to create steam in order

▲ **2.9** An insulated French press coffeemaker keeps your coffee warm all morning.

to froth the milk. These machines must have a safety valve to allow you to let steam escape, or you risk third degree burns.

If you dread going through the process of making a whole pot of coffee for just yourself, then you might consider the new **single-serving coffeemakers**. These machines work by forcing water through a prepackaged pod of ground coffee that looks like a tea bag. In about 90 seconds, coffee is ready. The pods can be ordered over the Internet or found at your local grocery store. The only drawback is that it makes a four-ounce cup, and most of us are used to larger portions. The average cup of coffee at a coffee shop is 12 ounces. That would be three pods, which quickly becomes quite costly.

TOASTERS AND TOASTER OVENS

Your basic toaster oven is still great for toasting and making open-faced sandwiches. But now it can also roast a whole chicken! First, assess your needs and the space you have to work with. Most people choose to have the toaster oven on the counter for easy access. If you have the option, you can get one that can be mounted under a cabinet. This frees up counter space if necessary.

Toaster ovens range in price from $60 to $300. Some of the more expensive models are insulated so the sides are cool to the touch. They also have adjustable racks, programmable touch pads, and convection capabilities. Decide what you are going to use it for and then make your purchase. No use making just toast in an oven that can cook a whole dinner!

Toasters, on the other hand, make toast. Decide whether you regularly need two or four slots, which will depend how many people eat breakfast together. The four-slot toasters come with a choice to use just two and avoid over-toasting. Also, consider toasters that have wider slots to accommodate bagels and other frozen "toaster" pastries. A removable crumb tray makes for easy cleanup. Consider the cool touch option, which can limit the chance of accidental burns.

MIXERS: HAND VS. STAND

For small, occasional mixing, a hand blender can work great. This style can whip up protein shakes or beat eggs quickly with minimum cleanup. It is also easy to store in a drawer. A typical hand blender is sold with three or four attachments, including different types of beaters.

Immersion blenders were once sold only to restaurants but have now hit the home market. An immersion blender is a wand with a long attachment that has a stainless steel blade at the end (**2.10**). You can immerse the wand directly into a liquid—like soup—and it will puree it instead of using a standing blender. Some come with other attachments like beaters and measuring cups. Look for one that has a variable speed.

For bigger jobs that involve large quantities of dry and wet ingredients, you'll need a **stand mixer**. The typical stand mixer looks intimidating but once you learn all its functions, you will want to use it often. Commercial-grade mixers now marketed to the home cook can beat eggs, grind meat, knead dough, grind grains for flour, and make homemade pasta! Common sense dictates that you start with the basics, like the whisk and beaters that mix, whip, and mash. You can always add the other fancy attachments later.

▲ 2.10 Immersion blenders are becoming more common in the home kitchen.

JUICERS

Juicers are like blenders on steroids. These machines are designed to extract juice from fruit or vegetables, creating a drink in the process. Some juicers also pulverize the entire fruit (including the peels) making delicious drinks with lots of fiber, an added health benefit.

THINGS THAT CHOP

A full-size **food processor** is a cross between a mixer and a blender. Basically, ingredients are pushed through a small feeder tube into a container that houses an exposed blade. When it hits the blade, the food is immediately chopped. How long you run the machine dictates the texture of the food. Salsa or gazpacho? It's just a matter of time. Small short bursts will give you a coarse chop. Run it continuously and you'll end up with a puree. The blade and speeds vary from machine to machine. This is one of those instances where a high-end name-brand product will last much longer than a lower-end product.

Coffee or spice grinders work the same way as food processors only they are much smaller. They have an exposed, stainless steel blade attached to a base where the motor is housed.

TOP ELECTRIC MINI-APPLIANCES

You can easily live without any of these machines but if you have the space and the budget, you should consider these time-savers.

Ice cream maker: Making your own ice cream is a romantic notion. However, ice cream makers are pretty pricey items, especially if you consider that you are probably not going to be using them every day. They can range from $50-$300.

Rice cooker: Ever wondered how restaurants make perfect rice every time? You can too with this electric device that cooks loads of rice, and even potatoes, quickly and easily.

Can opener: A great time-saver, but these machines get very dirty eventually, and are difficult to clean. If you want to get something off your countertop for a sleeker look, this appliance should be the first to go.

Electric frying pan: Who doesn't love fried food? Need we say more?

Waffle maker: The perennial wedding gift. If you didn't get one then, you probably don't need one now. However, waffles are a perfect fast and nutritious breakfast.

Electric grill: Thanks to boxing superstar George Foreman, these once dated pieces of equipment have made a comeback.

Slow cooker: Another machine making a comeback, the slow cooker is reintroducing a whole generation to pot roasts! Just put in all the ingredients, set the time and come back later for a home-cooked dinner and no dirty pots to clean. Great for busy families.

Bread machine: A whiff of fresh bread in the morning is very enticing. Bread machines require little culinary skill except proper measuring, and even that is done for you with manufactured mixes found in the grocery store. Auto shut-off and quick bread cycles are top features to look for.

Fondue pot: Another blast from the past, the new electric fondue pots can help create a fun family night meal. Get everyone involved in cutting and chopping and then eating and dipping.

Electric tortilla maker: Once you've tasted homemade tortillas, you'll never go back. Look for one with a non-stick surface and auto-temperature features. It's as simple as placing a dough ball in the center while the machine presses it and cooks it for you. It also does double duty making pitas, focaccia, and crepes.

When the lid is placed on the base and pressed down, the blade turns on. By holding the lid down, different consistencies can be achieved. The longer you hold it, the finer the grind will be. These are handy little machines that are great not only for grinding coffee but also spices and zests of fruit, like lemon.

There's nothing worse than starting a recipe only to find out that you don't have the right tools to complete it. You mustn't overlook the proper tool for a specific task: it really will make the difference between enjoying or hating all aspects of cooking. When shopping for tools, hold them in your hand to see if you can grip them properly. Some manufacturers make oversized rubber handles for their tools, which prevent slipping. On the other hand, don't put rubber-handled tools in the oven—you'll get a gooey mess!

Cookware

Cookware is a true kitchen investment: it will last a lifetime if you take care of it properly. You don't need many pieces—probably three or four pots and three or four sauté pans in varying sizes will do. Cookware choices depend on your cooking style, namely how hot you want your pots and pans to get. This is called "conductivity." Fancy terms aside, the heat from the energy source (in this case, gas or electricity) needs to travel from the cooktop through the pan to the food.

The type of cooktop you own will also determine what cookware to buy. Heed the following guidelines:

▶ Induction cooktops require magnetic cookware. See the previous chapter for details.
▶ Halogen, radiant, or smooth ceramic glass surfaces require flat-bottom cookware, which will distribute the heat more evenly and decrease hot spots in the pan.
▶ Gas cooktops, especially commercial grade, call for using heavier cookware to prevent scorching due to the great amount of heat emitted.

REACTIVE METALS

The chemical processes that occur when food is cooked determine the outcome of your dish. When heated, some metals react negatively with certain foods, and this can have an adverse affect on the flavor. Nonetheless, these materials still have a place in your kitchen because they are excellent conductors of heat. It just depends on how much time you are willing to devote to keeping

TABLE 3.1
Types of Cookware.

Type of cookware	What to look for	Oven safe?	Broiler safe?	Reactive?	Recommended how to clean	Comments
18/10 Stainless steel	Stainless steel over aluminum core or copper core	Yes, at high temp	Yes	No	Hand wash with mild soap, use a non-abrasive cleanser/pad when needed.	Expensive, but will last with care.
Aluminum (unlined)	Various weights of aluminum	Yes, at high temp	Yes	Yes, with acids	Soak immediately, then hand wash or use the dishwasher. Can use steel wool.	Great heat conductor, inexpensive, but can dent easily, absorbs foods.
Copper	Copper core lined with stainless steel/nickel	Yes, at medium temp if lined	No, if unlined	Yes, if unlined	Hand wash with mild soap, polish with copper polish or a paste of flour, salt, and water.	Expensive, best heat conductor if used with moderate heat, will last a lifetime. Must polish exterior.
Cast iron		Yes, at very high temp	Yes	Yes	Wipe out food with damp cloth, keep thin coat of oil on surface to prevent rust.	Inexpensive, can take the heat, great for searing, can rust if left in water.
Non-anodized/ aluminum	Hardened aluminum fused together	Yes, at medium temp	No	No	Hand wash with warm water, soap, and non-abrasive pad as needed.	Expensive, good for low-fat cooking.
Non-stick		Yes at medium temp	No	No	Hand wash with warm water, soap, and non-abrasive pad. Dishwasher safe.	Inexpensive, use with lower temps, non-stick surface will break down eventually.
Porcelain enamel	Porcelain enamel over cast-iron core	Yes, at high heat	Yes	No	Hand wash or dishwasher safe.	Expensive, very heavy, enamel can chip, good for low heat stovetop.
Hard-coat enamel	Porcelain enamel over steel core	Yes	Yes	No	Hand wash or use dishwasher, not abrasives.	Expensive, non-porous, heavy, food sticks easily if not careful, enamel can chip

them in good working condition since they are higher maintenance than non-reactive cookware (those pots and pans that won't react with any foods). To maintain the life of your cookware, you can't go wrong with hand washing. Anything baked on can be soaked in a solution of water and baking soda for fifteen minutes and wiped away. Never put cast iron or copper in the dishwasher, but stainless steel pots and pans will do fine.

Aluminum: Aluminum is a high conductor of heat and fairly inexpensive to buy. Unfortunately, if it's not covered with a top layer of stainless steel it reacts with acidic foods like lemons or tomatoes, which can make your meals taste metallic. Since it's also a soft metal, it pits, scratches, and stains easily. It's also hard to clean because the food bakes on quite easily.

Copper: Copper is a high conductor of heat. Some chefs swear by their pure copper pots. But these are professionals who have assistants to clean up after them! Copper is a soft metal, will scratch or dent easily, and needs to be polished. Copper pots are either lined or unlined depending upon their use. Unlined copper pots are great for making candy because they withstand very high temperatures. But unlined copper pots shouldn't be used to cook any acidic food since the metals can leach into the food, adding all sorts of unpleasant flavors. The interior is usually lined with tin, stainless steel, or nickel, which makes them very pricey. And after all that, they can actually wear out, so the pots might need to be refurbished (more money!). But you don't have to give up on copper pots altogether. The better, more expensive lines of stainless steel come with copper cores.

Cast iron: Cast iron conjures up images of campfires and old-fashioned stove cooking. It's been around for a long time and with good reason. It is an excellent conductor of heat and relatively inexpensive. These pans are heavy, and you probably won't be using them daily. But you just might—a pan that can withstand the most extreme heat will come in handy. Because they are so dense and conduct heat so well, they are the best at browning meats and poultry. Considering that they can be used easily either on the stove or in the oven makes it worth having one, too. A 10" skillet is about as big as you'd want, due to the weight of the iron. Cast iron pans are mildly reactive to acidic foods, like tomato and lemon juice.

To give it a non-stick surface, cast iron requires an initial seasoning. You can do this by coating the pan with a thin layer of vegetable oil and putting it in the oven for an hour at 350 degrees. For cleanup, just wipe out the pan with a damp sponge: never soak your pan in water because it will rust. With proper care, cast iron will last a lifetime: you can pass your "granny" pan down to your kids!

NON-REACTIVE COOKWARE

Non-reactive cookware is safe to use with all foods. It is usually easier to clean and doesn't require extra effort to keep it looking beautiful. Once the pan is cool enough to touch, just clean it with baking soda and warm water. Check out the bestselling metals in this category.

Stainless steel: Stainless steel is a form of iron and, by itself, not a good conductor of heat. Typically, this type of cookware has a metal core made up of copper, aluminum, or a combination of these, which is sandwiched between two sheets of stainless steel. This creates cookware that is easy to clean, resists rusting and denting, and is pleasing to the eye. There are extreme price ranges in this category: buy the best you can afford because they will last the longest. Make sure the core metal is not only on the bottom of the pan but continues up the sides. This will eliminate hot spots and make for even cooking. Stainless can be put in most dishwashers safely.

Non-stick surfaces: These pots and pans are usually made of aluminum that has a special coating, like Teflon, which prevents food from sticking. This makes for easy cleanup. However, the coating usually lasts only a few years and then the entire pan will need to be replaced. Cooking foods like scrambled eggs in non-stick cookware is a good choice because you can cut out the butter and keep your fat grams in check. Baking in non-stick isn't a great idea because you can't use anything metal to cut and serve the food: metal utensils will scratch, ruining the non-stick surface. Most non-stick cookware isn't made to be used with oils, which tend to leave a sticky residue. To make your cookware last, hand washing is recommended.

Anodized aluminum: The top layer of aluminum on this type of cookware has been chemically altered through an electrical

Boxed Sets: Buyer Beware

It might be tempting to purchase a set of one particular brand because it's cheaper than buying one pot at a time. However, this practice is not recommended until you've actually used one of the products and understand how it performs in your own kitchen. Most cooks find that each type of cookware has its advantages and disadvantages, so they usually own a combination of different types to meet their needs. You might end up with a whole set that just doesn't suit you. Worse, when the sets advertise "15 pieces," they're not talking about 15 pots and pans—they include the lids as individual pieces and often include pieces that you wouldn't buy or ever use! A better idea would be to stock up on the brand you like best when it is on sale.

process. This creates an extremely hard surface that is resistant to corrosion and abrasion. It is an excellent choice in place of traditional non-stick, since it is usually well-crafted and can last much longer. It will definitely be pricier, too. As with non-stick, hand washing is recommended over the dishwasher.

Enamel: Enamel cookware is made of some type of metal (probably cast iron or aluminum) and coated with porcelain enamel. It can't be heated as hot as other metals so it's appropriate for low-heat dishes like stews and soups. The enamel can chip easily if dropped or dinged. Since enamel cookware does retain heat well, you can use these attractive pans from the stovetop straight to the buffet. The downside is that even an empty enamel pot is so heavy that you'll need to start weightlifting just to pick it up. Imagine if you had to move one that was full!

BAKEWARE

As the name implies, bakeware goes inside the oven. These pieces need to retain even higher temperatures for longer amounts of time. Read through this list before you purchase, and think of the meals you usually cook before investing. You'll probably need three to four pieces in varying sizes in this category as well. Choose a mix of rectangular and square pieces, with sides that are at least three inches high. A typical baking pan will last a lifetime so, just like cookware, buy one piece and see if you like it before investing in an entire set. Consult you dishwasher's guide for which metals it can handle. Typically, aluminum, steel, and stainless steel are safe for the dishwasher. It's recommended to hand wash tin, cast iron, and disposable aluminum pans.

Metal: Metal bakeware is usually coated or uncoated aluminum or steel—metals that hold and distribute heat best for both short and long baking times. Look for silicone-coated bakeware that you can toss in the dishwasher for easy cleanup.

Porcelain: Usually glazed, porcelain is valued for its pure white properties. When fired, it becomes very hard and strong, making it ideal for baking, broiling, and cooking in the oven, on the stovetop, and in the microwave. The glazed surface is

A Note About Handles and Heat Transference

The handles on your cookware are just as important as the choice of materials. Handles should be riveted securely to the pan or pot. Depending on their composition, they may or may not get hot while cooking. Some handles are rubber, which are easy to grab but can't ever be placed into the oven for a quick finishing broil (they would melt). Ever wonder why some handles have holes at the ends? Handles with a hole disperse heat faster than solid ones.

naturally smooth, giving it non-stick properties. After cooling, you can also store it in the refrigerator or freezer.

Glass: Most glass ovenware is a combination glass/porcelain product since glass by itself is prone to break under extreme temperature changes. Glass retains heat well, so it is great for oven use. Cakes baked in glass pans have excellent crusts and brown evenly. It is virtually non-stick and easy to clean. It's safe for storing in the refrigerator or freezer; just be sure to let it cool completely first!

Stoneware: Stoneware is pottery that has been fully glazed and fired at high temperatures. It ranges from highly stylized manufactured sets with matching glass or plastic tops to more rustic pieces that are made of unrefined clays. Some stoneware manufacturers have produced lines that are attractive enough for serving.

Earthenware: Not to be confused with stoneware, this bakeware is made of glazed or unglazed pottery that is used for slow cooking stews and meats. Unglazed earthenware is also known as "clay pot cookers." Some manufacturers require that the pieces be soaked in water prior to cooking to prevent them from cracking in the oven. They may also need to be seasoned with oil first and then baked. This type of bakeware will eventually darken and spot with use. If you're pressed for time, this isn't the cookware for you. It's hard to remember to soak your pot (which can take up to four hours), and the slow cooking time can dampen your enthusiasm.

Silicone: Developed in France in 1982, silicone bakeware is a technological breakthrough that has come into the mainstream. The product is a flexible, non-stick material made of a combination of silicone and fiberglass. Manufacturers have reproduced virtually every shape of bakeware into a silicone counterpart. Some product lines safely heat to 500 degrees, and the pans are cool to the touch the minute you take them out of the oven. The molds are bendable, durable, and very easy to clean with just water and soap. Certain products are a must-have, like the baking sheet liner that makes a superior replacement for parchment paper. Shallow molds work better than deeper molds because silicone doesn't retain heat as well as metal.

The drawbacks of silicone are few but important to remember. Some recipes may yield uneven results until you modify them according to your oven. Silicone bakeware can be manufactured from various formulas, thus there is no uniformity to the product and results can vary from line to line. The products that don't contain a fiberglass element will not brown food as well as the ones that have it. You can't broil in them—they'll melt. And never use a sharp instrument to remove the food—it will cut the mold.

MUST-HAVE COOKWARE/BAKEWARE SHAPES

Sauté pan: The sauté pan is extremely versatile. The sides are either straight up or slightly curved and can reach up to 4", much taller than a skillet (**3.1**). This pan is designed to quickly cook foods in liquids. It's perfect for curries, pasta sauces, or any one-pot dish that has a combination of cooking steps. Start with a 3-quart pan with heat-proof handles, and a lid with a heat-proof knob or handle.

Skillet (8", 10", or 12"): The slightly curved sides are much shorter than a sauté pan's (**3.2**). The lower edges allow moisture to escape and ensure a crispier product. It also lets you reach in easily and turn the food over. Skillets are known by various other names, including a deep fryer or an omelet pan. It's good to have both stainless steel and non-stick versions of these on hand. Skillets usually do not come with lids.

Saucepan (1, 2, or 3-quart capacity): The small saucepan has tall sides and is ideal for cooking sauces, baked beans, and gravies. The larger saucepan is better for making pasta, soups, and stews. The straight bottom allows for even heating and reheating (**3.3**). Saucepans usually come with lids.

Stockpot (8, 10, or 12-quart capacity): This pot is large and tall; it's used to cook foods like soup when you don't want the water to evaporate. Most cooks find that a 10-quart stockpot will work for most recipes (**3.4**). Make sure to get one that has a pasta and/or a steamer insert if possible. This is a colander that allows you to strain the pasta and keep the water on the stove instead of having to lug the hot, boiling water to the sink. Stockpots usually come with lids.

▲ **3.1** Start your cookware collection with a 3-quart sauté pan with heat-proof handles.

▲ **3.2** Make sure to have 8" and 10" skillets on hand.

▲ **3.3** The straight bottom of a saucepan allows for even heating.

▲ **3.4** A 10-quart stockpot will work for most recipes.

Dutch oven (6, 8, 10, or 12-quart capacity with heatproof handles): The pot is similar to a stockpot, only shorter and wider (**3.5**). It comes with a tight-fitting lid that traps the moisture inside. It is used for braising or stewing meats. The wide bottom allows vegetables to be added in one layer. You should be able to transfer a Dutch oven into the oven. It is also referred to as a braising pan.

▲ **3.5** A Dutch oven is shorter and wider than a stockpot.

▶ **3.6** Most cooks are familiar with the basic roasting pan.

Roasting pan: This rectangular pan is made to hold large pieces of meat. It also has large handles that can withstand high heat and make it easier to carry when it is loaded up (**3.6**). The same type of pan can be used for lasagnas and other dense baked pasta dishes.

Double boiler: A double boiler looks like two saucepans that fit one on top of the other (**3.7**). The bottom pan is filled with boiling water while the top pan holds the ingredients. The hot water actually heats the bottom of the top pan. It's essential for melting chocolate and delicate sauces (like cheese) that scorch easily. You can create your own "double boiler" by using two slightly different sized saucepans.

▲ **3.7** A double boiler is used for heating delicate sauces and liquids.

Broiling pan: This is a shallow roasting pan with a rectangular sheet on top. The top sheet has large slots and ridges that allow fat and juices to drip from the meat as it cooks (**3.8**). The slotted sheet can be very difficult to clean, so try to get a steel one that has non-stick attributes. A broiling pan often comes with your oven, and it may be made of a metal material that can be put through the self-cleaning cycle.

NICE EXTRAS

Any of these specialty pans are nice additions to your larder of kitchen products.

Griddle: A griddle can be square, rectangular, or circular. It's completely flat with the tiniest edge and one long handle or two shorter handles across from each other. It's designed to cook foods with little fat, like pancakes. Low sides allow easy access to the food (**3.9**). Larger griddles can cover two burners at the same time, which is really nice if you are feeding a crowd.

3.8 The slotted top part of a broiling pan helps cook meats leanly and with less danger of a grease fire.

Grill pan: Relatively new to the scene, this pan is similar to a griddle, only the sides are taller. It usually has a non-stick surface and a long handle. Ridges mimic the grill marks of traditional barbecue grates so that when they are very hot they can sear your meat or poultry (**3.10**).

Cast-iron skillet: A well-seasoned cast-iron skillet can be very useful for making food that needs to be highly heated, like blackened catfish. If the pan is seasoned properly, you can cook with little or no fat.

▲ 3.9 The low sides of a griddle make it easy to turn your food.

Wok: Originally from Asia, a wok is a steep-sided pan that looks like a large salad bowl. The bottom is flat or round (flat is required if you have an electric stove), which allows you to cook food at high temperatures quickly. The high sides are useful for stirring while frying so that the food doesn't fall out of the pan, hence the term "stir-fry." Don't bother with non-stick or electric woks, they don't get hot enough. Anodized aluminum or carbon steel are better choices.

FOR YOUR BAKING NEEDS

Many home cooks know that baking is tougher than regular cooking. To be a successful baker is to be a scientist. Baking is more precise than other cooking techniques because it requires that ingredients are measured exactly for the recipe to work. Baking recipes may use different ingredients, but the bottom line is usually a combination of leavening agents and liquids. In addition, baking requires equipment that can stand up to the constant, dry, penetrating heat of the oven.

The good news is that you don't have to spend a fortune on bakeware to be successful. Bakeware is remarkably non-

▲ 3.10 A grill pan adds ridges so your food looks like it's been barbecued.

technical. Use the following guide to figure out what you need.

Cake pans: Cake pans come in a variety of shapes and sizes. Most recipes will specify exactly the sizes you will need. Here are a basic few to buy: two 10" round (layer cakes), 8" square (brownies), 9×13" rectangular (sheet cakes).

Spring form pan: This is a special pan that has a flat bottom with a removable ring that acts like the sides of a regular pan when the clamp is closed. When you are finished baking, just release the spring and lift it out of the way (**3.11**). The cake will still be on the bottom part and can then be frosted, decorated, or moved to a cake platter. These types of pans are ideal for making cheesecakes or flourless tortes that would be impossible to take out of a traditional cake pan.

▲ **3.11** A spring form pan lets you make cakes that would be impossible to remove from a regular cake pan.

Cookie sheet: Traditional cookie sheets are made of aluminum or steel and can have a non-stick surface. The latest rage in cookie sheets are the silicone mats placed on special pans. Stay away from non-stick and insulated cookie sheets; they are just not necessary, especially if you use parchment paper, which is always recommended.

Bundt pan: This is a 3½"-tall circular cake pan with a tube in the middle. It can have smooth or fluted sides. A bundt pan was all the rage in the 1970's. Today it's most commonly used for making angel food cake, but you can make many cakes in this creative shape (**3.12**). This is one of the few baking pans that should be non-stick since removing the cake can be difficult.

▲ **3.12** A bundt pan is excellent for angel food cakes.

Muffin tins: Muffins come in all sizes, and so do their pans. You can get regular muffin tins, mini-muffins tins that produce a bite-sized treat, or a special-occasion muffin tin, shaped like hearts, for instance. There are also specialty tins that create only muffin tops so you can treat your friends to just the best part!

Pie pans (glass/metal/ceramic): The best pie pan is one that heats up quickly, retains heat, and browns the crust. Hands down, oven-proof glass pie pans are the best. A metal pan should be on the heavier side and have a dark finish to help with browning. Ceramic pie dishes are nice when you want to present the pie to the table.

Gadgets, Gadgets, Gadgets!

All budding chefs discover a valuable lesson when learning to cook: it's all about having the right equipment. You are going to need a lot of small items to complete your kitchen tool collection. There are virtually millions of things you could buy, so you need to be judicious in your choices. What follows is a list of tools and gadgets that are used for daily cooking and baking. These basics should get you through just about any recipe, hopefully unfrazzled.

KNIVES

Knives are a chef's most important tools. A good set of knives will last a lifetime, so it's important to select ones that will make cooking easy and enjoyable. When shopping for a knife, go to a specialty cooking store where they will let you try them out. It's the only way to find out how the knife cuts and whether or not it's a comfortable fit in your hand. The number of inches used in the name of a knife refers to the length of the blade without the handle.

What Makes a Great Knife?

The best knifes are forged from carbon or high-carbon stainless steel. The forged blade is stronger and heavier than its stamped counterpart and the price tag will reflect that. The best knife is one whose tang extends all the way to the end of the handle. New technology has also produced knives made from a combination of ceramic and metal, like titanium or zirconia. These blades are supposed to be almost as hard as diamonds. These knives could be additions to your knife collection but

▲ **3.13** The chef's knife is an important all-around cutting implement.

▲ **3.14** A paring knife allows you to safely cut small items.

▲ **3.15** The serrated edge of a bread knife grabs thick or delicate surfaces.

stick with the basics first. The following are the basic knives you need to own:

Chef's knife (5-12"): The chef's knife is an important one and you need to know how to use it properly. If you want to see all the neat things it does, just turn on any cooking show and watch the chef work. Chances are he or she is wielding a chef's knife. The blade is quite broad and narrows at the tip (**3.13**). This design allows you to chop without your hand hitting the cutting board. The handle should feel heavy in your hand, but you should be able to balance it easily if it rests on two fingers extended. The smaller version is called a **cook's knife**, which is an excellent replacement for those who are scared of the chef's knife due to its intimidating size.

Paring knife: The blade is short, usually no more than four inches long, which allows you to hold a food, like fruit, in your hand and cut it without jabbing yourself. Use it for cutting small items like grapes, cherries, de-pitting olives, peeling an apple, or cutting a hunk of cheese (**3.14**).

Serrated bread knife: Mostly used for cutting bread, this long knife has a jagged or serrated edge that cuts through thick crusts or delicate fruit that might squish, like tomatoes (**3.15**). A serrated edge never should be sharpened because the actual cutting surface is protected by each small serration. Some companies create an entire set of serrated knives, but the bread knife is the classic that you can use for other foods as well.

Utility knife: This all-purpose knife can have a straight or serrated edge. It has a narrow handle and usually a four- to six-inch long blade. It handles all slicing, cutting, and dicing and can substitute for a chef's knife. It would be the knife to pick for making carrot sticks, or just about any job in the kitchen (**3.16**).

Meat cleaver: An impressive looking knife, this has a large, rectangular blade. It is quite heavy and uses the weight of the knife to cut through bone (**3.17**). It's great for taking off chicken wings. A **Chinese cleaver** is shaped like a cleaver but is the size of a chef's knife. It's easier to handle, but because it's smaller, it cannot be used to cut through bone. However, it can be turned over and the back used to break bone.

▲ **3.16** A utility knife is also a great all-around cutting implement.

▲ **3.17** A meat cleaver is heavy enough to cut through bone.

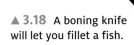

▲ **3.18** A boning knife will let you fillet a fish.

Boning knife: This knife is similar to a utility knife in size but will have a more flexible blade that can slide along a piece of fish and de-bone it, leaving the meat alone (**3.18**).

Grapefruit knife: Curved inward at the edge, this knife has either one or two serrated edges that allow you to remove sections of the citrus fruit without the bitter membrane attached.

Kitchen shears: Scissors specifically made to cut up poultry (**3.19**). Find a pair that can be pulled apart and dropped into the dishwasher to sanitize when you are done.

▲ **3.19** Kitchen shears make easy work of cutting up chicken and turkey.

Storing and Sharpening

Properly storing and sharpening your knives allows you keep them in tip-top shape. A dull knife is an accident waiting to happen. Why? You use a lot more pressure to slice something if the knife is dull and then it can slip and you're back to take-out for a week while your thumb heals. There are four basic sharpening tools but you only need to buy one.

Sharpening steel: This is the tool that looks like a big metal stick (**3.20**). To use it, swipe your knife across it once or twice

▲ **3.20** Sharpening steel will keep your knives in good working condition.

each side, sliding the blade down as you go. This will realign the edges of the blade, but not sharpen it.

Electric sharpeners: Electric sharpeners range from $60 to $300. Several ceramic or diamond composite disks rotate very quickly as you draw the knife over them. They are relatively safe to use, but you run the chance of oversharpening and damaging the knife. A **hand sharpener** works on the same principle as the electric sharpener—it's just not electric!

Sharpening stones: You can still sharpen your knives with the old-fashioned technique using a stone called whetstone. Two popular types of whetstones are composite rectangular blocks made up of silicone carbide or abrasive particles of diamonds bonded on a plate of steel. For each of these, the stone has to be lubricated with either oil or water to retard heat buildup during sharpening.

If the stone has two sides of different coarsenesses, start with the coarsest side and finish with the finer side. Start with the heel of the blade (the part closest to the handle) at the back of the stone and hold it at a 20-degree angle. Gently guide the entire knife away from you, making sure to make contact with the stone and the blade. Turn over and repeat on the other side. Continue with this motion all the way down the blade of the knife. Some people like to swipe five or six times, some people like to swipe twenty times. Less is more until you learn about your knives and how they react to the sharpening. You don't want to take away too much of the steel at a time. Then use the sharpening steel to realign the edges of the blade. This will also remove any loose bits of metal.

CUTTING BOARDS

Cutting boards come in all sizes and materials. Wood and polyethylene cutting boards are very forgiving, and will help maintain the sharpness of your knives. Wood is also naturally antibacterial but has to be hand washed. Polyethylene can be thrown in the dishwasher. Glass and ceramic boards are very hard on knives so they are not recommended. Flexible cutting boards are great to have in addition to regular cutting boards.

The flexibility lets you funnel ingredients easily. Cutting boards all need to be thoroughly washed in hot soapy water after each use. It's best to designate a cutting board for different food groups and avoid cross-contamination. Definitely use different ones for cutting raw fish, poultry, or meats!

BASIC UTENSILS

Colander: Colanders drain liquids. Some come with expandable handles that suspend them in the sink. Look for a sturdy base or feet if you need hands-free access.

Dry measuring cups: Get a cup (or set of cups) with a thin, even rim so you can smooth over the top easily for an accurate measure.

Fat separator: Fat separators look like liquid measuring cups, but the spout is connected near the bottom instead of at the top. When the fat rises to the top, the liquid on the bottom can be poured off, minus the fat. This tool is indispensable for making gravy.

Funnel: A cone-shaped tool used to direct a large amount of ingredients into a smaller vessel.

Hand grater: Grating requires a lot of effort so your grater needs to have very sharp edges and a comfortable handle. A **box grater** has four surfaces, each with a different type of grater.

Ladles: Ladles are like small bowls with long handles. They come sized by how many ounces they hold. A six-ounce is quite large for transferring soup. A **batter ladle** has a small lip for easy pouring.

Liquid measuring cup: This cup needs to be see-through, easy to read, easy to clean, and accurate. Glass or plastic work well, just make sure the plastic is heat-resistant.

Measuring spoons: This set should include a tablespoon, 1 teaspoon, ½ teaspoon, and ¼ teaspoon measurements. They usually come in a set, linked together.

Mini bowls: Tiny bowls that can hold pre-measured ingredients.

Mixing bowls: These are the workhorse of the food prep process. They usually come as a set of three or four, and it's a great bonus if they come with plastic lids.

Pasta server: A perforated claw-like ladle that "grabs" the spaghetti.

Skimmer: A mesh strainer attached to a long handle, it's used to skim fats off the surface of soups and stews while cooking.

Slotted spoon: A perforated spoon used for straining solids from liquids.

Spatulas: Spatulas have a long handle with a rectangular flat head. They are used for scraping bowls and folding ingredients. You'll need at least a small (2" wide) and large (4" wide) spatula in a flexible material, most likely rubber or silicone. Make sure the spatula is stiff enough to wield heavier batters and doesn't collapse on itself. If you have room, it's best to stock more than one because sometimes timing requirements don't allow you to clean up!

Strainer: A strainer is made of mesh and usually has a handle. Use this instead of a colander when the ingredients are smaller.

Tongs: Tongs are used to grab and transfer food. A 12" stainless steel pair will handle most tasks. Get one that has a clip to lock it closed for easy storage. Use nylon tongs if you cook with non-stick cookware.

Vegetable peeler: A good peeler can handle most vegetables from carrots to squash.

Whisks: Whisks are indispensable when you want to whip air into liquid, such as scrambled eggs or making whipped cream.

Wooden spoons: Look for ones with long handles; they won't scratch your pots and pans, and won't melt. Just be sure to wash them in hot water and air dry them because the heat from the dishwasher can split the wood. You're apt to use three, maybe four spoons when cooking a full course meal, so buy several of your favorites.

Zester: A metal peeler that will take off the outer skin of citrus fruits without the white pith (the bitter part).

■Extra Extras

Here's a list of things that might be fun to own, although they're not required for you to be a successful cook:

Bagel slicer	Corn butterer	Nutcracker
Baster	Corn holders	Pizza wheel
Bottle opener	Duck press	Potato ricer
Bottle stopper	Garlic press	Salad spinner
Butcher's twine	Ice cream scoop	Salt & pepper shaker(s)
Can opener	Kitchen scale	Skewers
Cheesecloth	Meat pounder	Spoon rest
Cheese slicer	Meat thermometer	Sushi mat
Cherry pitter	Melon baller	Timer
Chopsticks	Mortar & pestle	Tortilla press

Everyday Dinnerware

Your everyday needs for plates, glasses, and silverware are different than when you are entertaining. Select patterns that you won't get sick of, and try to match them to your kitchen colors or style. For your plates, open stock assortments allow you to buy only the pieces you want, and are a good choice over boxed sets. They are often easier to replace when things get broken. However, don't count on any pattern to be around forever. Whatever you choose, make sure it's good quality, and that it's dishwasher safe. If you have small children, melamine is an ideal choice because it is virtually indestructible.

Utensils should be 18/8 or better stainless steel for everyday endurance. Before you buy, hold the knives and forks in your hands to make sure that the weight and angle of the design are comfortable for you. Choose a pattern that will go from breakfast to dinner seamlessly. Avoid wooden handles and other hard-to-clean metal accents, and those that are not dishwasher safe.

Glasses should be heavy enough to withstand everyday use. Avoid thin rims that shatter readily. Make sure the mouths are wide enough to drink from comfortably. An assortment of 16-, 8-, and 4-ounce glasses are perfect for all occasions.

For a family of four, consider buying the following:

8–10 dinner plates	12 salad forks
8–10 salad plates	12 dinner knives
6–8 cereal bowls	12 soup/cereal spoons
6–8 rim soup bowls (wider and flatter)	12 teaspoons
6–8 small snack bowls	8–10 16-ounce glasses
6–8 small snack plates	8–10 8-ounce glasses
12 dinner forks	6–8 4-ounce glasses

■Linens

No kitchen is complete without the tools that actually protect the cook. I always cook with an apron on—it gets me in my chef mood quickly and protects my wardrobe too! The items on this list are must-haves:

Aprons	Dish towels	Pot holders
Dishcloths	Oven mitts	

Organization: Use It or Lose It!

Today, just the *word "organization" is a selling feature. We have stores, catalogs, and TV shows devoted entirely to organizing your life. Having too much stuff, not being able to find what you need, and swearing that you'll clean up one day is no way to live. Clutter actually stifles and impedes everyday activities. The kitchen is no exception. It will be impossible to prepare great meals and entertain if your surroundings are in disarray.*

Most kitchens are located by the back entry, whether it's the side door to the house or the garage. Thus, the kitchen becomes the drop-off place for keys, purses, backpacks, sports gear, and the like. If your kitchen is out of control, it's time to smarten up and get a plan. If it's possible, make a habit of keeping things that don't belong in the kitchen out of the kitchen; this will make cooking and eating much more enjoyable. Since kitchens are the most expensive room in the home per square foot, the first order of business is to maximize space and minimize chaos, the standard goals of organizing.

The kitchen can be divided into the following zones that suggest an organized approach to it all: prep and cooking, clean up, eating, and food storage. Granted, work areas will overlap in a small kitchen and there should be plenty of space in a large kitchen. But the basic principles will hold true for all kitchens, and yours is no exception.

To get started, make a list of all the drawers and cabinets you have. Make a note of what doesn't work. No need to make yourself crazy and move something from a spot if you like where it is. Just concentrate on the aspects that drive you crazy.

The hard part comes next. Take out all your kitchen gear and inventory it into the same four categories. Then go through, piece by piece, and decide where it will go. This is also a great opportunity to throw out anything that is chipped, broken, missing a piece, or not functional in any way. Don't hang on to anything that you don't use. Make a list of all the items that need to be replaced, like a scorched wooden spoon, then chuck them! This way, you can be assured you'll be replacing your items with better functioning and more attractive new ones. Once you've culled your stuff down to what you are going to keep, you need to arrange it according to your work zones. Remember your four piles? Each pile needs to be put away in the proper zone. Once you have the kitchen organized in this detailed manner, you'll find cooking a lot more enjoyable. Here's a guide for what should go where.

The Prep Zone

The word "prep" is short for preparation. In a professional kitchen, there is a "prep chef" whose main job is to prepare ingredients for the cook (the person that actually cooks the food). The prep area needs to be clutter-free at all times. It's daunting enough to begin cooking, and there's nothing more frustrating than having to clear the newspapers and push things aside just to get started.

The prep area should provide easy access to knives, cutting boards, kitchen tools, and bowls. Start by standing where you want to prep and designate a drawer to have all the peelers, hand graters, presses, slicers, shredders, choppers, etc. grouped together. On the counter, you may want to have a utensil container. Be creative: this can be any container or piece of pottery that matches your décor. Just make sure it is large enough to hold everything so it isn't a struggle to take things out when you need them.

Also, get an attractive container like a wicker basket with a flat bottom. Here you can keep all your oils, vinegars, and non-perishable sauces at hand right on the counter to avoid making multiple trips to the pantry. Having them all in a container also allows for easy cleaning.

Most kitchens have a variety of drawers and cabinets. Deep drawers in the prep area can hold bowls as well as mini-appliances. Cabinets above should hold your baking dishes. The ones used less frequently should be placed at the top. Don't stack heavy things too high or on top of it all. Put the heaviest and least used items, like large casserole dishes, on the bottom of the stack. If possible, don't stack too many things together unless they're a set. It's too easy to have an accident and for something to crash down on your head. If space limitations require tall stacks, organize them by shape.

▲ **4.1** A magnetic rack can store knives and keep them handy at the same time.

◼ Knife Storage

Knives need to be kept in a rack or block to prevent them from getting damaged by other knives or hard objects. A block placed on the counter gives you quick, easy access to them as you cook. Have an extra drawer? Place an insert specifically designed for knives into the drawer. If you're lacking counter space or drawers, invest in a magnetic rack that can hold them on the wall under your upper cabinets (**4.1**).

The Cooking Zone

In many kitchens, the cooking area may overlap the prep space. I use the area closest to my oven as the designated cooking zone. Here you should have access to everyday pots and pans. Additional cooking utensils, like wooden spoons, ladles, and tongs should be placed in drawers near your stove or cooktop.

The cabinets or drawers near your stove could hold all your pots and pans. Group items according to use, with those used more frequently in front. Ideally, it would be great to keep the lids on each pot so you don't have to go rooting around for them. Space limitations sometimes preclude this from happening. So the next best thing is to organize them in groups, and store the smaller pots inside the bigger pots.

There are various ways to tackle the lid problem. One way is to place them in a rack holder specifically for lids. They can then be placed on a half-shelf in the back of the cabinet, on a roll-out extension to the side of the door, or actually mounted on the door.

Large pans and skillets should be placed next to pots and pans. Occasional-use items could be put under the half-shelf near the rear. If you have large drawers in your kitchen, make sure not to overload them with too much weight because it could damage the glide mechanism. A narrow cabinet is ideal for storing baking trays and cutting boards. It can also be handy for oversized serving items.

Hanging a pot rack is a storage option if you have a small kitchen or just like the look. However, pot racks only look good if the pots are shiny and new looking. Who wants to stare at a junkyard in the middle of their kitchen? So you should either buy beautiful, high-quality cookware or be prepared to diligently maintain your cookware's appearance (**4.2**).

ORGANIZING SPICES

People who love to cook have lots of spices. Your biggest obstacle is finding the one you want quickly. Spices need to be handy and easy to reach in order for you to even remember which ones you own. Since they are highly perishable, spices need special consideration regarding storage as well. A dark, cool place is optimal. Here are some options.

4.2 A pot rack adds to a kitchen's appearance but the pots need to be kept in good shape.

Group spices alphabetically: Obviously, finding a spice in this manner is easy, since we all know our ABCs. Also, if there is more than one cook in the house, the system is easy to figure out.

Group spices according to cuisine: This is a more advanced and subjective way of organizing your spices, but it's a great time-saver if you find yourself preparing the same dishes over and over. Let's say your family loves Italian food. It makes more sense to have all the necessary spices grouped together for one easy grab.

Display and storage options for spices are endless. Drawer racks can hold as many as 16 to 30 bottles. Designating a cabinet near the prep or cooking zones is another option. If you have a built-in microwave, the cabinet above it is a great place to put a double-decker lazy Susan, where you can store more than 50 standard spice bottles. If there is clearance, mount additional racks on the doors. If that's not enough room, an under-cabinet pull-down shelf can hide even more!

If you don't have a free cabinet to use, you can purchase an attractive stainless steel or chrome rack that can display your spices on the wall or counter. Prepackaged spices purchased in carousels are a popular option, often given as gifts. The drawback is that there is no way to know how fresh the spices are and replacement bottles may be hard to find. Yet another option is to use stackable clear containers. Print a label with each box's contents and adhere it to the front (**4.3**). Use either the alphabetical or cuisine classification system for easy searching.

■Organizing Small Appliances

While cooking, you'll need your gadgets, but not necessarily all the time. Remove any appliances that you seldom use from your countertops. The less you see, the neater things are, the more organized you'll feel. Starting to get the picture?

THE OFTEN OVERLOOKED CORNER

Most kitchen counters have one or more corners to deal with. This often large, cumbersome space under the counter is a source of frustration because it's hard to access all the items that it can actually hold. If you leave everything on top of the counter and stash it in the corner, it just looks ugly. But an appliance garage might be the perfect solution. An appliance garage can keep the blender, food processor, or electric can opener at arm's reach but out of sight. Shutting the door of the garage will also simplify the design of the space, making it more appealing. A typical corner garage is 16¾" W × 18" H × 11¾" D—roughly 1½ square feet. Before you buy or build one yourself, make sure that your appliances will fit within these dimensions.

NOT-SO-LAZY SUSANS

Lazy Susans are just about the most functional organizing tool out there (**4.4**). They make reaching into the back of a cabinet a snap. Depending on the size of your cabinet, choose the diameter of the circular shelves, probably between, 18"–28" round. The shelves come mounted on a pole that can be anchored in the center of the cabinet, and they are designed to turn independently. If your cabinet is angled, the shelves can be full circles. If your cabinet is a traditional corner, you need to use three-quarter circles, called kidney-shaped. Otherwise, the circles would hit the door.

◀ **4.4** A lazy Susan makes it easy to access items in a cabinet.

The Cleaning Area

It's pretty obvious that eating and cleaning make up 90 percent of what people do in the kitchen. Set the table, clear the table, do the dishes, put them away—sound familiar? Since these two activities go hand-in-hand, let's maximize efficiency and minimize the hassle.

Your dishwasher is probably installed close to your sink. If possible, designate the drawers for your flatware to be near the dishwasher as well. The top drawer should hold eating utensils. The second drawer should hold large serving utensils. The third drawer should hold potholders and trivets. The fourth drawer can hold placemats, napkins, and dish towels.

Plates and glasses need to be close to the dishwasher as well. The cabinet above the dishwasher works great. Store the plates on the bottom shelves to reduce arm strain. Consider installing a wall-mounted plate rack for daily-use plates. Put glasses on the upper shelves or in the next cabinet (**4.5**).

Chances are that you make coffee every day, so set up a coffee station that has all the things you use. Put sugar cubes and sugar substitutes in small containers, coffee stirs in a ceramic holder. Keep filters handy, hidden in an adjacent cabinet. Consider placing all the items on a decorative lazy Susan. Invest in a "tree mug" to display your collection on the counter or put mugs in the cabinet above the coffeemaker.

CLEAN UP TIME!

With a little thought, cleaning up can occur efficiently and effortlessly, getting the job done quickly so you can return to more pleasant pursuits. The cabinet under the sink is usually relegated as the spot where cleaners and extra trash bags are thrown haphazardly. An under-sink container or pullout wire system will keep all your cleaning supplies organized (**4.6**). If you install it yourself, make sure it doesn't interfere with the garbage disposal or pipes. Dish towels or paper towels can be mounted on a rack right on the door.

The countertop around the sink is a natural place for things to collect. Avoid cluttering up your sink area with cleaners and sponges. A nice ceramic container can hold most of these things, as long as the contents can dry completely. New plastic containers with suction cups can hold sponges and sponge brushes directly on the sides of your sink. Install a mop and broom rack inside a long cabinet or behind a door.

▲ **4.5** Store heavy items like plates on the bottom shelf, with glasses above.

■The Quick List for Under the Sink

Baking soda	Glass cleaner	Silver cleaner
Cleaning rags	Hand soap	Sponges
Dishwashing soap	Paper towels	Trash bags
Electric dishwasher soap	Scouring powder	

TRASH

If you don't have a designated cabinet for your trash bin, under the sink is usually a good spot for it. Install a gliding rack to make it easier to throw out large items. Place trash bags next to the bin. Freestanding trash cans are also available. The most sanitary option is a stainless steel can with a hands-free lid that opens when you step on it.

The Eating Area

Hopefully, all the stuff in the kitchen has found a home. Now you can find your kitchen table! The eating area should be completely clutter-free. Take everything off the table before every meal. If you eat at an island counter, this rule is even more important. No one can enjoy a meal when they are surrounded with odds and ends. Make your meals peaceful by putting away distractions.

▲ **4.6** Under-the-sink wire pullout systems can help you keep things organized.

Food Storage

Putting away dried goods is always a lesson in organization. The best method lies in customizing the interiors of your drawers and cabinets. If you are renovating your kitchen, virtually all cabinet manufacturers offer different options for making food storage easier. If you're not replacing your cabinets, you can purchase interior fittings from a variety of online and catalog home-improvement retailers. Before purchasing anything, make sure you understand how it works, ease of installation, if it will fit in the cabinet you are considering, and if it is worth the money.

THE WALK-IN PANTRY

A traditional pantry is ideal because it groups all your food together away from your equipment and allows you to easily view and maintain your stock. Store food that is used daily at eye level. Stepped shelving will allow you to store much more food, and makes finding what you own easier. Label bins and baskets that are stacked higher up with seldom-used items. Don't forget about the door. Buy a hanging shoe organizer for smaller items that may get lost. Collapsible mesh bins can store perishable food and be put away when not in use.

PANTRY CABINET

If you don't have a separate walk-in pantry, then the next best option is a pantry cabinet. This is an oversized cabinet, preferably placed near the refrigerator and designed specifically for food storage. Pantry cabinets often have pullout drawers so you can easily find what you are looking for. All of the suggestions for a walk-in pantry apply here as well.

If you don't have a pantry cabinet, don't despair! This is the time to pull out all the stops and be creative. Make one by installing pull-out shelves in a regular cabinet with doors. It's important to measure the amount of clearance you'll need between the shelves so space is not wasted or too crowded for easy access. Don't forget the storage possibilities on the door. Racks can hold lots of bottles and small cans.

INVENTORY CONTROL

Organizing your food goes a long way towards keeping shopping to a minimum and the cooking running smoothly. If you know where things are, filling out a grocery list is a snap. Keep a running list of frequently used items on the refrigerator, and a separate list near the pantry. Or install a dry-erase board on the back of your pantry door or on the inside of one of your cabinets. This way you can easily jot down the items as you finish them.

If you're computer savvy, there are some great programs that can generate all kinds of shopping lists. Grocery list programs use shortcuts that avoid retyping frequently used items, which saves lots of time. They can even keep track of the price you paid and what store you found something in. The lists can either be printed out or downloaded to your handheld device!

Here is a starter grocery list to help you create your own.

Grocery List

Qty.	Produce/Fruit	Qty.	Produce/Veges	Qty.	Dairy	Qty.	Nuts/Dried Fruit
	Apples		Artichoke		Cheese		Almonds
	Bananas		Broccoli		Cottage cheese		Apricots
	Blueberries		Carrots		Cream cheese		Cashews
	Cantaloupe		Celery		Eggs		Cherries
	Grapes		Cucumber		Milk		Cranberries
	Honeydew		Green onions		Mozzarella		Peanuts
	Oranges		Lettuce		Non-dairy cream		Prunes
	Peaches/nectarines		Onions		Sour cream		Raisins
	Pears		Potatoes		Yogurt		Walnuts
	Plums		Sweet potatoes				
	Strawberries		Tomatoes				
	Watermelon		Winter squash				
			Zucchini				

Qty.	Meat	Qty.	Cold Cuts	Qty.	Drinks	Qty.	Drinks
	Beef		Deli ham		Bottled water		Orange juice
	Chicken		Deli roast beef		Club soda		Sports drinks
	Pork		Deli turkey		Coffee		
	Turkey		Hot dogs		Cranberry juice		
	Fish		Salami		Grape juice		
	Shrimp				Lemonade		

Qty.	Canned Goods	Qty.	Crackers/Bread	Qty.	Supplies	Qty.	Supplies
	Applesauce		Corn chips		Aluminum foil		Scrub powder
	Black beans		English muffins		Coffee filters		Tall kitchen bags
	Cannenelli beans		Hamburger buns		Dishwash soap		Tissues
	Chilies		Hot dog buns		Freezer paper		Toilet paper
	Mandarin oranges		Potato chips		Napkins		Trash bags
	Olives		Pretzels		Paper plates		Wax paper
	Pineapple		Water crackers		Paper towels		Zip gallon bags
	Tomato sauce		Wheat crackers		Plastic wrap		Zip quart bags
	Tomatoes, diced		Whole wheat		Scrub pads		Zip snack bags

Qty.	Frozen Foods	Qty.	Frozen Foods	Qty.	Condiments	Qty.	Condiments
	Frozen broccoli		Chicken fingers		Honey		Oil
	Frozen corn		Pancakes		Honey mustard		Olive oil
	Frozen green beans		Pizza		Jelly		Peanut butter
	Frozen mixed veges		Sausages		Ketchup		Preserves
	Frozen peas		Veggie burgers		Maple syrup		Salad dressing
	Frozen spinach		Waffles		Mustard		Salsa
					Non-stick spray		Vinegar

■Organizing Your Food

Grouping food types is a matter of preference, but there are some general rules to follow:

► Canned foods should be stored together, organized by contents for quick access. All the beans together, all the fruits together, etc.

► Dry items such as beans, pastas, rice, and boxed quick meals should be stored together.

► Store all baking ingredients together. Place larger bulk flours, sugar, baking mixes, and cake mixes in a bin or basket. A small bin should have decorating tools like icing tips, food coloring, nonpareils, and cupcake holders. Another bin could have baking soda, baking powder, extracts, powdered sugar, and brown sugars. Unless you're baking every day, put the bins on a top shelf. Now it's just a quick grab and go for making cookies because you aren't running around getting all the ingredients.

THE REFRIGERATOR

Most refrigerators create a love-hate relationship with the food you've purchased. You go to the store, you spend a lot of time picking it out, falling in love with it, dreaming of how you will use it in your next great meal and then, boom. When you get home, there's no room to put anything, you find old produce that's spoiled, and you can't reach the items you need, much less find them.

Most people don't put any thought into organizing the refrigerator. For it to work properly, it needs to be managed daily. Start with small changes that can make a big difference in keeping food fresh, thus lowering your grocery bill, too.

Let's start with the refrigerator door. Manufacturers have installed large shelves that can store gallon jugs on the door. Unfortunately, that's inefficient for two reasons. First off, the door is too warm. It's exposed to the air too often. Beverages can't remain cold enough. Secondly, with all that additional space, the door has become a great place to contain all the random condiments that used to gather in the dark recesses never to be seen again. So move the milk into the interior of the fridge, and put taller bottles like ketchup and marinades in the door.

Now, let's tackle the shelves. Don't hesitate to adjust the shelf heights to accommodate your personal tastes. Place the first shelf about 6–8" off the bottom. Since the lower part of the refrigerator is the coolest, store yogurts, butter and cream, and any small perishable items (like eggs). Behind them store items that need to be refrigerated but aren't accessed daily.

The next shelf should have 16–18" between it and the shelf above it. (Make sure the space between the shelves is high enough to fit a gallon jug with room to get it out easily.) This is where milk and orange juice will go. If you must store beverages in the door, store soda cans and bottled water. These have a longer shelf life.

The next shelf is where all cooked food should be placed, including take-out containers and leftovers. If you have invested in the rectangular stacking system, you'll be able to store as much as you need. Glass containers with rubber lids can go from oven to refrigerator without a glitch.

This leaves about 6" left on the top. Most medium size jars average 5" (salsa, mustard, jelly, etc). If you install a lazy Susan on this shelf, you'll never have to reach into the back again (**4.7**).

◀ 4.7 Refer to this illustration for the optimum set-up for your refrigerator.

The drawers in the refrigerator are designed to hold perishable food, such as fruits, vegetables, and deli meats. Some drawers come with adjustable humidity that helps keep produce fresh. Designate one for vegetables and separate the fruit. Line the drawers with paper towel to absorb any juices that may accumulate from overripe items.

General Organization

Organizing has never been more fun. Whether you use handcrafted wooden products or funky neon plastic ones, storage systems bring a sense of order and control. Getting organized frees you up to be creative and happy in your kitchen. So invest in systems that you can get excited about. Check out dollar stores and warehouse centers, even supermarkets for great ideas.

BASKETS, BINS, AND CONTAINERS

Baskets, bins, and containers can be used in any of the kitchen zones. So what's the difference? Baskets provide easy access to items and keep them tidy on the shelf. Use small baskets for small items: drinking straws, napkins, wooden stirs, cookie cutters, sugar substitutes, tea bags, bouillon cubes, coffee filters, and salad dressing packets. Larger baskets are ideal for large items: linens, cleaning supplies, small appliances, table accessories.

Bins differ from baskets in that they don't usually have a handle and one side, usually the front end, is lower so items are easily accessible. Before you buy, analyze how the stacking system works. Take time and check the stability of the entire stack after the bins are loaded on top of each other. Check to make sure that they are easily stacked and secured to each other. Some systems are just better designed than others. The best choice is a set that clicks together or one where a flat bottom surface of the bin actually sits on top of the bin below it. Also, make sure the bins are durable and washable.

The world of containers is endless. Matching canisters or containers come in various sizes or can be purchased in sets. Things that match are visually satisfying and will at least give the illusion of organization! Pick a set that has colors that match your kitchen. Square canisters are better than round because you have less unusable space between them. Also, see-through canisters are preferable over opaque. Why? Easier to find stuff.

An important consideration when buying a container is how well it will keep your food fresh. Food that can become bug-infested needs to be stored in airtight containers. Containers with lids that lock or create a vacuum seal are the best. Baskets, bins, and containers come in all sorts of materials, which of course have their pros and cons.

Plastic/plastic composites: Inexpensive and available in fun colors. See-through, easy to clean, and cheap to replace. Most stackable systems are plastic. However, plastic isn't as elegant as some other choices, and can break or crack when dropped.

Vinyl coated wire: Inexpensive and easy to replace. However, once the vinyl cracks, it's ugly and can rust. Not good for storing cleaning supplies where water might be an issue.

Woven organic material (like wicker): This choice has a rustic quality about it. Cheap ones don't last; they tend to unravel. Consider lining them with fabric or a dinner napkin for added protection and a custom look.

Metal: Has an industrial look or can be painted custom colors. The downside is that you can't see through these, and metal bins can scratch, dent, or rust with heavy use. If you choose this option, make sure you can properly label them.

Glass: Ideal for storing food because items can be identified easily. Glass can be washed safely in the dishwasher or put in the refrigerator.

Organize Your Recipes

If you like to cook, chances are you have a pile of magazines, newspaper clippings, and copies of recipes cluttering the counter or desk in your kitchen. Now is the time to sort, purge, and file them. The following method combines the best of two popular systems. For recipes that you've never cooked, use the portable file method. It's quick and easy to maintain. Once a recipe has been cooked and rated as a family favorite, transfer it to a three-ring binder. This eliminates losing favorites or coming across an old recipe and wondering if it was good.

STEP ONE: THE PORTABLE FILE

Place all clippings in a portable file system with dividers. Use headings such as appetizers, breakfast, meats, pasta dishes, side dishes, desserts, and soups. When you tear out a recipe, promptly file it! Smaller pieces of paper should be taped on copy paper. If you plan to cook it that week, write down the ingredients you need and place the recipe in the front divider under the heading "This week's meals." After you cook it, don't forget to mark down any adjustments to ingredients, cooking time, or omissions. Lastly, grade it. Our family has a grading system on all new recipes presented at dinner: once a week, once a month, once a year, once in a lifetime! If it's a "once in a lifetime" rating, toss it! If it was a winner, write the rating, date, and year cooked, and move on to Step Two.

STEP TWO: THE THREE-RING BINDER

Mount all recipes on copy paper using tape or a glue stick. Place each recipe in a plastic sleeve. Use dividers with headings similar to the portable file to sort them. Flipping through this book will be easy, and the plastic keeps the recipes splatter-free. Encourage other family members to browse the book and help plan meals.

Projects That You Can Do

If your kitchen *needs some updating, the right approach may be simpler and more affordable than you think. If you are tired of your cabinets, change their look by painting, faux finishing, and replacing the hardware. Sew a window valance and matching placemats or new seat cushions. If you just want to add some fun accessories to the kitchen, try making some decorative crafts like a mosaic lazy Susan or a menu board.*

The following are big-picture projects that are extremely easy to implement. If you are the least bit crafty, you can find hundreds of design books for accessory ideas that match your style. Look to these books as well for a decorator's color palette choices, depending on the style you've chosen.

Paint Is More Than Color

Color greatly affects the mood of a space. Warm colors, like orange, red, and yellow, fill up a space and make it seem friendly and inviting. Cool colors, like blue, green, and purple open up a space and make it feel calming and expansive.

All of the main design elements can be painted, including the kitchen walls, cabinets, and floors. Since kitchens are inherently busy places, it's best to simplify the color palette of the entire room to one or two colors that either complement or contrast. If the flooring is dark, change the walls and cabinets to lighter colors, preferably in the same tones.

■ A Word on Safety

As with any project using machinery, paint, chemicals, or power tools, always wear safety goggles, follow the products' instructions, keep the room well ventilated, and dispose of chemicals properly according to local regulations.

FAUX FINISH WOOD FLOORS

Floors are tricky to paint. In order for the paint to be sealed properly, you have to spend days without going into the kitchen. For busy households, it's just not feasible. Not only that, but it's easy for crumbs and dirt to be sealed along with the paint. However, the results can be remarkable. If you're still game for painting the floor, use a technique like whitewashing or pickling, which will add subtle color to the surface and won't get ruined by extensive traffic.

Whitewash Pine Floors
Clean your floors, making sure there is nothing left on the surface. Using a brush, apply a whitewash stain on a small

area. Let it set for a few minutes. Use a rag to work the stain into the wood along the grain, wiping any excess as you go (**5.1**). When it's dry, coat with a clear, water-based finish.

Pickling Oak Floors

Clean your floors, making sure there is nothing left on the surface. Using a brush, apply a pickling stain to a small area. With a rag, work the stain into the wood against the grain, wiping up any excess as you go (**5.2**). When it's dry, coat with a clear, water-based finish.

PAINTED SISAL FLOOR RUG

It's easy to customize a rug for your kitchen floor with stencils and a hand-painted border. Purchase inexpensive sisal rugs or remnants at a home improvement center or carpet store. Find a pattern or color in your kitchen to carry over to the carpet (**5.3**).

Materials:

Old sheet to cover the work surface	3" paintbrush
Inspirational design pattern	Ruler
Carbon paper, chalk, or a stencil	Painter's tape
Sisal carpet, medium weight	Acrylic paint

Instructions:

1. Using chalk, draw a design or transfer a design by tracing it on top of a piece of carbon paper (the image will transfer wherever you push, so be careful). You can also use or make your own stencils.

▲ **5.1** Whitewash stain adds a nice rustic look to pine kitchen floors.

▲ **5.2** Work the pickling stain into the wood after you brush it on.

◀ **5.3** A customized sisal rug makes your kitchen truly your own.

2. Paint the design, making sure to cover the spaces between the weave. If you are working with stencils, you can use spray paint, which may give you better coverage.
3. Measure and tape off three inches from the border of the rug.
4. Paint the border with a 3" brush.
5. Remove the tape and let it dry for 24 hours.

FAUX FINISHES FOR THE WALLS

If you are looking to create a focal point, you can paint an accent wall. Dramatic results can be achieved using paint and glaze combinations. Try out different combinations on a piece of poster board before you start on the walls. For large areas, it's better to pick an easy-to-do technique because large areas take patience and skill to complete. That said, mistakes are relatively harmless and easy to fix; just wipe them off and start over.

Sponging

Sponging is the easiest and most fun painting technique to try because you really can't make a mistake. Using a sea sponge, dab one or several colors on the wall in a random pattern. Keep in mind it's best to choose colors that already exist in the color

▲ 5.4 Start by painting your kitchen wall a base color.

▲ 5.5 Use a sponge to apply the lighter color to the base coat.

palette of the room. Start by painting the walls a base color and let dry (**5.4**). Cut the sea sponge in half so that you have a flat side to use. Cut one half further into halves for smaller pieces. Wet the sponge, wringing out extra water. Start with the darkest color and dip the sponge into the paint. Press the sponge on the wall lightly but firmly (**5.5**). Don't drag or rock the sponge. Continue until the sponge needs more paint. Let dry. Layer more colors if desired. Sponge lighter colors on top.

Combing

If you want to have a tailored look without committing to wallpaper, combing can give you a similar effect (**5.6**). By dragging the comb down the wall, pinstripes of color are left

◀ **5.6** Combing is an unusual technique that creates a great contrasting wall.

▲ **5.7** Ragging makes the space softer and more intimate.

behind. Additional horizontal stripes create a basket weave effect. To start, pick two colors. Paint the walls with one color as a base coat. Mix the second color with one part paint to five parts glaze. Using a roller, apply the second color in a three-foot section, top to bottom, in one continuous motion. While it is still wet, drag a large comb or wallpaper brush through the glaze. Straight lines will give you a tailored look, wavy lines will give a quirky, fun look.

Ragging

To soften a room's overall texture, ragging instantly makes the space more personal and intimate (**5.7**). There are no hard edges because the rag creates cloud-like swirls of paint. Like sponging, you can't really make a mistake. To start, get a clean soft rag, preferably lint-free. Pick two colors; the base color should be lighter than the top color. Paint the walls with the base color. For the ragging effect, mix the top color with one part paint to five parts glaze. Dip a damp, scrunched up rag into the paint and apply to the wall. A natural pattern may appear that you can mimic or just apply freely as you want.

PAINTING LAMINATE COUNTERTOPS

Laminate countertops are easy to paint provided that you prime them first. The primer needs to be specifically made for non-porous surfaces. Make sure to open up the windows for ventilation. Sealing is time-consuming but necessary to prevent the paint from scratching off at the slightest pressure (**5.8**).

Materials:

Medium grit sandpaper	Water-based latex house paint
Non-porous primer	Paint roller
Brush	Polyurethane sealer

Instructions:

1. Sand countertops with medium grit sandpaper.
2. Prime using a paint roller. Let dry overnight.
3. Paint surfaces, using two coats of house paint. Let dry completely between coats.
4. Coat with five coats of polyurethane. Follow the manufacturer's instructions carefully.

◀ **5.8** After priming the counter, paint it with latex paint.

PAINT AND DECORATE TILING

Colors can date a kitchen, so your tile may be in great condition but of the wrong era. Or it may simply not reflect your personality or the warmth you want your kitchen to project (**5.9**). If you choose to paint a tile surface in your kitchen, which could include the floor, countertops, and/or backsplashes, keep in mind that the kitchen is a high traffic room. Anything you do needs to be sealed properly (which means you can't use it for at least a day) or you'll find all your hard work chipping or peeling.

Materials:
Ceramic or porcelain tile
1 cup of water with a tsp vinegar
Chinagraph pencil
Variety of ceramic enamel paint colors
Several good quality detail brushes
  such as #3 round
Acrylic sealer

▶5.9 Hand-painting a backsplash can update a kitchen or simply add personalization and zest to it.

Instructions:

1. Wash the tile with the vinegar and water solution.
2. Air-dry completely.
3. Using the Chinagraph pencil, draw a design onto the tile. If you cannot hand-draw, look for appropriate stencils.
4. Paint the design, starting with the largest areas first. Let dry.
5. Paint smaller details.
6. Using the smallest brush, outline elements for accents.
7. Seal with acrylic sealer.

Concealing Less-Than-Perfect Cabinets

Cabinets define the kitchen space more than any other element. There are some crafty things you can do to change your cabinets with a little creativity and ingenuity. For example, if you are stuck with cabinets in a color you've grown to hate, simply painting them can make a huge difference. And, since the variations are endless, this is where your personal style can shine through!

Below is a general guide to get you started. More specific instructions for techniques can be found at a local paint store. Before you pick your final colors, purchase a quart of one or two colors that you like and test them out. It's surprising how different colors look in the actual space than on a small swatch.

Try one of the following techniques on your cabinets and see what a difference it makes. All surfaces need to be prepped before painting. The difference between a professional-looking job and an unprofessional one is usually the time spent on stripping, sanding, filling, and priming the surface of the cabinets. Don't skip any steps! The end result will be worth it. Read through the instructions several times before attempting any of these finishes. Make sure you fully understand what you need to do, and have the right tools and equipment on hand before you start.

DISTRESSED FAUX PAINTING TECHNIQUE

Also known as "shabby chic," distressed cabinets give a kitchen a country theme and a timeworn feel (**5.10**). There are many variations of distressing, ranging from super peeling to only slightly worn edging. Use a high pigmented paint to form the base coat. That color will be an accent color in the final product.

▲ **5.10** Distressing gives cabinets a country look; this cabinet projects a timeworn feel.

Materials:

High pigment color paint, one base coat color, one top coat color
2" paint brush
Wax candle
Medium grit sandpaper
Fine grain sandpaper
Matte acrylic varnish
Newspaper or drop cloth

Instructions:

1. Cover the floor with a newspaper or drop cloth.
2. Prep the surface to be painted (strip, wash, sand, fill, etc. as needed).
3. Using a 2" brush, apply colored paint to the cabinet using crisscross strokes.
4. Allow it to dry.
5. Liberally apply wax on the edges of the door, raised moldings, and some flat areas.
6. Apply two coats of top coat color using long, even strokes. Let dry between coats.
7. Rub sandpaper where the wax was applied, removing the wax.
8. Sand the entire cabinet with fine grit sandpaper.
9. Seal with matte acrylic varnish.

▲ **5.11** Hi-gloss cabinets add a modern effect to your kitchen décor.

HI-GLOSS LACQUER

Lacquered cabinets instantly create a modern look, and this technique works best on plain-front cabinetry. Since lacquer is a difficult paint to work with, you can mimic lacquer using any high-gloss acrylic or enamel paint. Follow with a glossy varnish for extra shine and protection (**5.11**).

Instructions

1. Cover the floor with a newspaper or drop cloth.
2. Prep the surface to be painted (strip, wash, sand, fill, etc. as needed).
3. Remove the cabinet doors and place them on a flat protected surface. Using a paint sprayer, coat the surface with latex enamel undercoat (primer).
4. Allow to dry.
5. Apply at least two coats of color with a paint sprayer, using very thin coats.
6. Allow to dry completely.

▲ **5.12** Changing knobs and drawer pulls provides a quick and inexpensive makeover.

■Changing Hardware on Cabinets

Instantly change the look of your cabinets by simply replacing the knobs and drawer pulls. Many options are available from antique brass to high-tech stainless steel. Make sure to pick knobs that screw into the existing holes. If you have a two-hole pull, measure the distance between the holes (**5.12**). Better yet, take an old pull with you to pick out a new one that's the perfect size.

Crafty Kitchen Solutions

Not every project needs to be large in scale, you can enhance your kitchen with a few crafty ideas that are ornamental yet functional. Everyone can use more storage. To add some organizational elements, try building an island, installing a wall-mounted pot rack, or a backsplash tool bar.

CREATE AN ISLAND

You can easily make a kitchen island that is both attractive and serviceable. In this project, I've combined a ready-made shelving system with an MDF countertop to create the island (**5.13**). Combining 34½" high shelving with a ¾ top gives you the exact right height for a countertop: perfect for cutting and chopping! The shelves can supply a generous amount of storage space. You can even customize the shelving. Some can be designed to be wine racks. There are also metal baskets you can purchase that match the shelves. The length of the island will vary depending on the length of the shelving. The width of the finished island will depend upon how far apart you space the shelves. For the following instructions, I used 3 foot-long shelves and positioned them 4 feet apart to make a 3×4 foot island. For your version, measure out the space you'd like to allocate to the island, and then make a quick trip to your local home improvement store.

Materials:

One 4×8 piece of ¾-inch plywood, MDF (which has a smoother surface) or melamine—have the home improvement store cut your surface to the dimensions of your finished island

Two complete 13" × 36" × 34½" shelving units (which will hold up the top)

Fine grain sandpaper
Paint primer
Acrylic paint
Water-based acrylic varnish, matte finish
4" paintbrush
Varnish brush

▲ **5.13** A kitchen island is not very hard to make at all, and it will add storage and cabinet space.

Instructions:

1. Place newspapers on the ground and lay out the top. If it's wood, sand smooth with sandpaper.
2. Prime, let dry, and then sand again.
3. Paint with two coats of acrylic paint. Let it dry completely between coats.
4. Varnish with two coats of varnish. Let dry according to instructions. (Melamine will not have to be finished.)
5. To assemble, place the shelving units where the island will stand. Place wood on top of the top shelf of each unit. Adjust the shelves so that the edge of the top is lined up with the edge of the shelves. The top is easily removable.

MAKE A WALL RACK FOR POTS

You can attach this rack to a wall in your walk-in pantry or in the kitchen (**5.14**). Use your imagination when choosing a picture frame. It can be a sleek modern metal one from a frame shop or an old, carved wooden frame from a junk sale. Faux-finish the frame for further charm. The size of the picture frame should be determined by the amount of wall space to be covered.

Materials:

One large picture frame,
  at least 1" in width
Wire mesh, enough to stretch
  over the frame
Wire cutters
Flat ½" trim, smaller than the
  width of the picture frame trim

Handsaw
Finish nails
Staple gun
Hammer
Screw hooks
Screws and molly
S-hooks

Instructions:

1. Turn the picture frame over and spread wire mesh across the back.
2. Staple mesh to one side of the frame. Stretch it tightly across and staple it to the other side.

▶ **5.14** Keep your pots close at hand with this custom-built wall rack.

3. Trim the mesh with the wire cutter so it doesn't stick over the edge of the frame.
4. Nail trim to the frame, covering the cut edge of the wire mesh.
5. Nail screw hooks to the frame.
6. Turn over and hang, screwing the screws through the screw hooks.
7. Hang using screws and molly.

EASY BACKSPLASH ORGANIZER

Unlike most systems that require drilling into the backsplash, this rod is actually installed under the bottom of a cabinet (**5.15**). It turns an unusual space into a cool organizer. Purchase cooking tools that have a hook on the end of their handle or a hole that can be hooked on to the rod. There must be at least 18 inches under your counter to have enough room to hang larger utensils.

Materials:

Tape measure
Metal curtain rod, length determined
  by amount of space available

Screws
Screwdriver
Drill and drill bits
S-hooks, ½ size

Instructions:

1. To determine the length of the rod, figure out where the brackets can be attached. They will be screwed into the bottom of the cabinet, near the wall. Make sure it's unobstructed.

◄ **5.15** Store your cooking tools under a cabinet, within easy reach.

2. Mark the ends by penciling inside the screw hole of the brackets. Make sure they are each 1" from the wall.
3. Screw the brackets into the bottom of the cabinet.
4. Hang the rod and accessories.

MOSAIC LAZY SUSAN

By now, you're singing the virtues of the lazy Susan like a true enthusiast. To make one, you need to find a flat circle (**5.16**). A small wood tabletop sold at home improvement centers could work great. Some also sell wood or MDF lazy Susan surfaces.

Materials:

Vitreous glass tiles ¾" (18mm) square	Cement-based tile adhesive
One wood circle	Sanded grout
One lazy Susan mechanism	Latex gloves
Wood glue	Small crafter's sponge
Two clean soft cotton cloths	Tile sealant
	Paintbrush for sealant

Instructions:
1. Using carbon paper, transfer a design onto the wood. You can also make geometric designs if that's easier for you.
2. Spread the tile adhesive over the surface of the wood.

▶ **5.16** A mosaic lazy Susan is not only functional but can be beautiful!

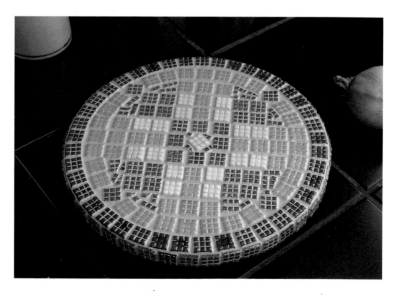

3. Gently press the glass tiles in the pattern. With a damp cloth, wipe away any adhesive that has gotten on the surface of the tiles.
4. Allow to dry for 24 hours.
5. Following manufacturer's instructions, mix the grout. It should be the consistency of oatmeal.
6. Put on the gloves and spread grout between the tiles using the sponge. Don't stop until it's all grouted.
7. Clean the sponge well and then go over the top of the surface and wipe it thoroughly. You may have to wash the sponge over and over. Wait 15–30 minutes and repeat until the surface is clean and the grout lines are even depth.
8. Let it set for 3 hours. Wipe with a clean cloth. Any hard particles can be carefully scraped off with a window scraper.
9. Allow it to set about a week before sealing. Follow the manufacturer's instructions on sealing.
10. Attach the lazy Susan mechanism to the circle by screws or using wood glue. Let it dry for 24 hours.

CREATE A UTENSIL HOLDER

With a little imagination and color, an old ceramic vase can be transformed into a pretty container that holds all your kitchen tools (**5.17**). Make sure to keep in mind the color scheme of your kitchen so it will blend in. The base coat should be a darker color than the top coat.

Materials:

Large ceramic vase
Water-based acrylic paint in
  two complementary colors
Sponge
Water
Two disposable plastic plates
Spray varnish

Instructions:
1. Pour paint on a plate.
2. Dip the sponge into the paint and gently dab color onto the vessel. How much depends upon how much of the original vase color you want to cover.
3. Let dry completely.

► **5.17** An old vase (center) can be a beautiful utensil holder.

4. Dip the sponge into the other color and continue dabbing in a pattern all over the vessel until it's satisfactory.
5. Let dry completely.
6. Protect the paint with a coat of spray varnish.

MAKE A TRIVET

A cute hot plate is always handy (**5.18**). These are easy to make and fun to use.

Materials:
One 6×6-inch ceramic or porcelain tile
Four small cork circles
One cup of water with a tsp vinegar
"Liquid nails" glue
Chinagraph pencil
Variety of ceramic enamel paint colors
Several good-quality detail brushes such as #3 round
Acrylic sealer

Instructions:

1. Wash the tile with the vinegar and water solution.
2. Air-dry completely.
3. Using the chinagraph pencil, draw a design onto the tile.
4. Paint the design, starting with the largest areas first. Let dry.
5. Paint smaller details. It's okay to cover some of the other paint colors.
6. Using the smallest brush, outline elements for accents.
7. Seal with acrylic sealer.

BEADED NAPKIN RINGS

These are really fun to make and they add a splash to an ordinary table setting (**5.19**). Memory wire will spring back into a coil, making it perfect for napkin rings. When picking out beads, select a variety of shapes and colors.

Materials:

Memory wire
Assorted glass, ceramic, and painted beads in various shapes and colors

Needle-nose pliers
Wire cutters

◄ **5.18** A trivet always comes in handy and it's not a bad gift idea, either.

▲ 5.19 These beaded napkin rings can be a conversation starter over dinner.

Instructions:
1. Cut the wire approximately 3 cuffs long (12" in length).
2. Close off one end of the wire into a loop with the needle-nose pliers. Create a kink at the open end so the beads won't fall off while stringing.
3. String the beads in an interesting pattern and then loop the end closed with pliers.
4. Let the wire return to its coiled shape. Insert cloth napkins.

SERVING TRAY DECOUPAGE

Leave this tray on your counter for a trip down memory lane or to surprise family members (**5.20**). It's fun to collect the photos to make the project, too!

Materials:

Collection of family photos	Scissors
Pastel copy paper	Foam brush
Decorative edging scissors	Decoupage medium
Wooden serving tray	Spray acrylic varnish
Sandpaper	Acrylic paint
Clean cloth	

▼ 5.20 This serving tray is especially nice when family and old friends come over.

Instructions:

1. Sand the tray. Wipe with a clean cloth.
2. Make copies of your favorite photographs. (Put the originals away—this way you will preserve them!)
3. Using the decorative edge scissors, cut out the photographs.
4. Working with one at a time, place paper photo cut-outs on top of the tray and brush a very thin coat of decoupage medium over the surface. Smooth out any air bubbles or wrinkles.
5. Continue to add pieces, overlapping the edges and angling the photos for an interesting layout.
6. Cover the entire tray, bending photos over the edges and smoothing them as you go. Any small exposed areas can be painted with acrylic paint.
7. Seal by spraying with acrylic varnish.

MENU BOARD

Both family and friends will get a kick out of this one. Nothing's as much fun as entering the kitchen and reading a chalkboard menu listing the day's dishes (**5.21**). Mounting it

◀ **5.21** Your family will always know what's on the menu with this handy board.

▲ 5.23 Seat cushions are easy to make from fabric remnants.

2. Double the material, and using the pattern, pin it to the material. Cut two pieces of fabric for each cushion to be made, reusing the pattern.
3. Turn one piece over and pin them together. The right sides will be facing each other.
4. Start sewing in the middle of one side and make your way around the entire cushion. When you get to the side you started with, turn the corner and sew it, but leave a 4" opening for turning the cushion inside out.
5. Trim the seams so they aren't too bulky.
6. Turn the fabric inside out and fill with fiberfill or cut foam.
7. Fold the seam at the opening to match the seam of the machine-sewn length and iron seams to get rid of any bumps.
8. Pin and hand-stitch the 4" opening closed using a hidden stitch.

6

Maintaining and Cleaning Your Kitchen

The best case *scenario is that your kitchen runs smoothly and a small amount of muscle keeps it clean. The worst case scenario is when you can't locate the stinky smell in the refrigerator, the garbage disposal keeps jamming, and grime has taken over every surface. Don't despair. This chapter is devoted to keeping your kitchen in tip-top shape. With some practice, it can be accomplished quickly and easily.*

Create a Plan of Attack

Maintaining a kitchen requires cleaning, disinfecting, and polishing. Cleaning involves getting rid of the dirt, crumbs, and grime of daily kitchen use. Disinfecting is getting rid of germs so you can avoid food-borne illnesses. Polishing maintains the finish of your equipment, surfaces, and tools.

Cleanliness is a relative term—a few crumbs on the floor send some people straight to the broom closet. Others prefer to just put on slippers and walk right over the crumbs. Perhaps you fall somewhere in between, cleaning as you go but avoiding the tough stuff. Experts would like to dictate exactly when, what, and how to clean every item in your kitchen. But one size doesn't fit all! Maintaining a routine that fits your comfort zone is of the utmost importance since you're more likely to follow a method that doesn't feel like an overwhelming burden.

If you break down all the jobs that need to be done, a clear plan of attack emerges. Since there are tasks that need to be completed on a daily, weekly, monthly, and yearly basis, cleaning can be broken down into levels.

Daily cleaning covers everyday jobs: washing the dishes, disinfecting countertops, cleaning the sink, sweeping the floors, emptying the garbage, and clearing up clutter. It's great to get into the habit of wiping up all spills when they happen. If you are pretty consistent with the daily tasks, then deeper cleaning will require much less effort. Keep in mind that most daily tasks can be accomplished with just a microfiber rag and water, perhaps a bit of cleanser. Don't pull out the big guns unless you've tried a weaker cleaning formula.

Weekly cleaning covers disinfecting and polishing (depending on how often meals are prepared). Most busy people can get away with keeping up with deep cleaning the sink and counters, mopping the floor, wiping down the refrigerator, cleaning the microwave, toaster oven, and cooktop, and dusting off window treatments and collectibles.

Monthly or quarterly jobs include cleaning out the refrigerator, the oven, descaling coffeemakers, wiping down wood cabinets and moldings, cleaning the windows, and sorting through the food supplies.

Annual cleaning covers the larger projects or jobs that are done as needed: resealing countertops, polishing silver, washing walls, cleaning out drawers and cabinets, reorganizing, and minor updates.

■ Get It Together

It's easy to tackle any job when you've got everything you need in one place. Put cleaners and detergents together in a bin. You'll use them more often if they are handy. Make sure they are stored safely out of the reach of small children. The cabinet over the refrigerator is the last place a child will look and it can be big enough to hold a medium-sized bin of supplies.

Supplies and Tools

It's tempting to purchase specialized tools that promise to make every cleaning job easy. Unfortunately, a lot of those don't work, break quickly, and become clutter. So don't waste your money! Stick with the essentials listed here:

Baby washcloths
Broom, store with bristles off the floor
Cloth diapers
Dust mop, disposable microfiber cloth systems beat
  the old-fashioned dust mop
Dustpan and handheld broom
Microfiber towels
Rubber gloves, great for sensitive hands
Scouring pads, nylon or plastic
Sponge
Steel wool pads
Stiff brush
Toothbrush, soft
Two large buckets, big enough to submerge a mop
Vacuum cleaner and attachments
Wet mop, buy one with a removable head that can
  be thrown into the washing machine

All About Cleaners

Cleaning solutions rely on the formula's level of acidity. Every household cleanser, from toilet bowl cleaners to dishwashing soap, is either acidic, neutral, or an alkaline, referring to a ph scale that ranges from 0–14. Low ph is acid, high ph is alkali. Water is neutral ph at 7.

Acids and alkalis clean different things. Acids remove soap scum and hard water, cut oils and buildup, and dissolve glue and tarnish. Alkalis work by removing grease and soap scum and are usually combined with a mechanical element like powder that involves more elbow grease.

Purchasing commercial products eliminates making your own but you'll pay a lot of money for the convenience. Also, storing all the single performance products can be cumbersome. That said, there's no guesswork involved—glass cleaner cleans glass! But are they worth the cost? Sometimes they are, like when only a petroleum-based product will do the job. Metal cleaners and polishers are another category that really should be store-bought. Making them involves purchasing hard-to-find ingredients; mixing the formulas involves handling toxic substances.

Environmentally friendly manufacturers claim to produce non-toxic cleaners by using natural ingredients that do not release harmful fumes. Guess what? Their formulas are based on all the same tried and true ingredients used for generations. If you want to make your own cleaners, there are some pros and cons to consider. The pros are that the formulas should be easy to mix, the ingredients should be inexpensive relative to store-bought cleaners, and you'll be bringing fewer toxins into your home. You can clean practically anything with baking soda, vinegar, ammonia, washing soda, chlorine bleach, and hydrogen peroxide.

The cons are few, but worth noting. When you trade the power of a synthetic chemical, be prepared to substitute elbow grease and increase the "spray and wait time." Also, just because they are homemade doesn't mean they aren't unsafe. Ammonia, chlorine bleach, and washing soda are very strong chemicals and dangerous when used incorrectly. For example, you should never mix chlorine bleach with anything. The result can cause toxic fumes that can kill you! Washing soda is a very strong alkali so use gloves to protect your hands. Ammonia has noxious fumes that some people can't tolerate. Don't forget to label all products immediately.

■Toss in the Towel and Toss out the Sponge

Disinfecting the kitchen is crucial to maintaining your family's health. Surprisingly, the first step is to throw out your sponge! Sponges tend to stay wet and harbor tons of bacteria. A great alternative is to use fresh dishcloths each day. Manufacturers have introduced multi-use throw-away scrub cloths that work with this purpose in mind. But they are costly. Instead, buy a bunch of infant washcloths. The baby washcloths are the perfect size for scrubbing dishes. They have a soft side for polishing and a rough side for scrubbing. They are so lightweight that they quickly dry between uses. Cloth diapers are useful for any cleaning chore in the house— and they are made to withstand years of washing! They are very soft and absorbent and can take the place of paper towels. When they are dirty, just launder and reuse. You can feel confident that you aren't cleaning a counter with a dirty sponge!

THE BIG FOUR

If you are going to make your own cleansers, you need the following four main ingredients (**6.1**):

Baking soda: A mild alkali that cleans and deodorizes practically anything. It's easy, fast, cheap, and healthy to use. Baking soda can clean all metal cookware without scratching the finish. Just wet the pan and sprinkle baking soda liberally. Scour with a nylon scrubber brush. Deodorize cutting boards and countertops by sprinkling them with baking soda. Spray with water, then polish with a cloth. Baking soda also removes residue from plastic containers, polishes tile and glassware, and removes black marks, crayon, and wax on surfaces.

White vinegar: A mild acid that cleans glass, mirrors, shines wood floors, and removes hard water deposits from surfaces. Just create a 50/50 solution of white vinegar and water in a spray bottle and use as needed. Vinegar also neutralizes soap residue and makes it easier to rinse off. Lemon juice and cream of tartar are other mild acid cleaners. They dissolve

▲ **6.1** You can make most of the cleansers you need with these four common ingredients.

mild rust stains and soap film, and can remove tarnish from brass and copper.

Ammonia: Some people use nothing but ammonia to clean. An alkali cleaner that works on practically anything, ammonia's fumes are really harsh. Don't clean aluminum with ammonia. Ammonia is best used when it's been diluted. A tablespoon of ammonia in a quart of water can be used to get grease off most items. Try soaking dishcloths in a small bowl of water with a teaspoon of ammonia while you clean the kitchen. Rinse and drip-dry on the sink and they will be clean for the morning.

Bleach: An acid cleaner that disinfects and whitens. Never use full strength. Protect clothing and hands whenever you are using or mixing this product. Chlorine bleach is the standard ingredient of most household disinfecting products. It kills most bacteria and doesn't leave a harmful residue that needs to be rinsed off.

Since chlorine is powerful and effective, there are plenty of commercial cleaners with chlorine bleach in them. They come in gels, sprays, and wipes. But you can make your own much cheaper. For disinfecting surfaces that come in contact with food, combine ½ teaspoon chlorine bleach with 2 cups of water. Wipe away all food particles, wash with hot soap and water first. Soak the surface for 3–5 minutes. Rinse and allow to air-dry.

Chlorine bleach isn't perfect. Its odor can be offensive to many people. It's not that great for septic tanks or the environment. It can also damage metals, so rinse them to avoid marring the finish. Chlorine also dissipates rather quickly. It's best to mix up a batch of cleaner as needed.

An alternative to chlorine bleach is **hydrogen peroxide**. Remember that little brown bottle tucked in the back of your medicine closet? It is an odorless disinfectant that kills viruses, bacteria, and mold. It's the mastermind behind all the oxygen cleaners and it's great if you want a non-chlorine product. To make your own cleanser, put full-strength hydrogen peroxide 3 percent solution in a spray bottle. Use on counters, sinks, and faucets.

Borax is another naturally occurring mineral that gives spectacular cleaning results. When mixed with other ingredients, borax controls alkalinity. It also eliminates odors and boosts cleaning power.

Castile soap is an all-natural soap made with vegetable oils (like olive oil or coconut oil) instead of animal-based fats. Found at many health food stores, it is used in homemade cleaning formulas in place of harsh detergents. Amazingly enough, when mixed with water and used as a cleaner, it leaves virtually no residue!

Yet another alternative is harnessing the power of herbs. Essential oils are made by extraction of certain cells in plants, usually a combination of the leaves, flowers, roots, and stems. They help protect the plant from injury and the environment. The essential oils of many different herbs provide natural protection against molds, fungus, bacteria, and even viruses. Natural antiseptics include pine, lemon, lavender, tea tree oil, and birch bark. Because they are highly concentrated, only a small amount is needed. Add 10–20 drops of any of these essential oils (available at local organic food stores) to your homemade cleaners to boost their power and create a great smelling product! Be sure to shake well before each use since the oils will separate. As with any herb, use cautiously and make sure that it's safe to use if you are pregnant or nursing.

The following formulas can be used to perform all the tasks in your kitchen:

All-purpose cleaner #1—Mix together in a spray bottle
¼ tsp washing soda
1 tbsp white vinegar
¼ tsp vegetable-oil-based soap
1 cup hot water
10 drops of essential oil of lavender
10 drops of tea tree essential oil

All-purpose cleaner #2—Mix together in a spray bottle
1 cup water
¼ tsp liquid dishwashing soap
1 tbsp baking soda
½ tsp borax

All-purpose scouring powder—Mix in a can with a perforated lid
1 cup baking soda
10 drops rosemary essential oil

All-purpose disinfectant—Mix together in a spray bottle
1 cup water
2 tbsp castile soap
1 tsp tea tree oil
8 drops eucalyptus essential oil

Glass cleaner—Mix together in a spray bottle
1 cup water
1 cup vinegar
10 drops of lemon essential oil

Porcelain polish—Mix together in small bowl
2 tbsp cream of tartar
½ cup hydrogen peroxide

Wood floor cleaner—Mix in a large bucket
3 tbsp castile soap
½ cup vinegar
½ cup black tea
2 gallons water

Wood cabinet cleaner—Mix in a squirt bottle
2 cups of water
2 tbsp vinegar
1 tbsp lemon oil

Floor Care

Like everything else that needs to be maintained, your kitchen floors can be put on a schedule.

Kitchen floors should be swept after every meal if possible, but at least once a day. Pick up any stray objects. Sweep or vacuum the whole floor. You might consider a stick vacuum for use strictly in the kitchen. If you are going to buy one, examine how it collects dirt. Usually, the dirt is sucked into a removable cup that needs to be emptied after each use. After a while, it can get really grimy and hard to clean. Another option is to dust the floor with a disposable microfiber cloth system. A new cloth is clipped onto the head of the duster each time you use it.

When you are done, you just toss out the cloth. The only drawback is the cost of the cloths. They are pretty pricey.

On a weekly basis, you'll need to mop. First sweep. Then mop. Avoid any mops that don't have a removable, machine-washable head. It makes no sense to use a mop with a sponge head that gets dirty the first time you use it—it just stays dirty until it's replaced. Mops with reusable washable microfiber cloths really capture dirt. Buy at least four cloths to use so that you always have a clean one.

The best way to avoid mopping with dirty water is to mop with two buckets. Fill one with water and cleaning solution. Fill one with water only. Dunk the mop into the bucket with detergent and ring the mop head until it's damp. Clean the floor and rinse the mop in the other bucket. When the rinse water gets too dirty, a quick trip to the sink for clean water is easy.

Different flooring needs different care. If the floor has been newly installed, follow the manufacturer's instructions, which can usually be found on their Web site. This will ensure the warranty stays valid. If your flooring predates you, follow these simple guidelines.

WOOD FLOORS

Unless your wood floor is fifty years old, it most likely has been refinished and sealed with a urethane coating. Frequent sweeping or vacuuming without a beater head will keep it clean and minimize minor scratching. For dirt and grime removal, a slightly damp mop coated with wood floor cleaner is usually all that's needed. Home remedies call for a cup of cold tea or vinegar in a gallon of water to help maintain a clean, shiny finish. Oil-based stains should be removed with a solvent-based wax because too much water can spot the wood.

LINOLEUM OR RESILIENT FLOORS

New high-end models are manufactured as no-wax flooring. If you have a recent no-wax resilient floor, this is one instance where purchasing the cleaning product recommended by the manufacturer and following the directions closely will save you time and money. Better yet, go to the Web site for detailed care information ranging from daily maintenance to stain removal. Most manufacturers want you to buy a specific no-rinse cleaner for the floor. Just a damp mop and a bit of floor cleaner is needed. Scuff marks, crayons, ink, glue, paint, and dried-on food can be removed safely with a little baking-soda-and-water paste. Time and use will eventually dull the finish, but chances are you'll be sick of the floor and want a change by then anyway.

If you are stuck with an old vinyl floor, first strip it using one cup of ammonia mixed with one gallon of water. Make sure to ventilate the room. When the mop shows signs of dirt, rinse thoroughly and continue until the water runs clear. Be prepared for this step to take a lot of time, especially if the floor is really dirty. When it's clean, let it air-dry for two to three hours.

Next, seal it with a floor sealer—a professional flooring product. Then apply a wax by hand buffing, similar to waxing a car. Sorry, there is no way around this step. For regular cleaning, don't use anything that contains ammonia. It will undo all your hard work. Just a cup of vinegar and quart of water should keep your linoleum floor shiny.

TILE OR STONE FLOORS

If the tile or stone is sealed, tile floors clean up really well with just plain water. If it's not sealed, put a sealer on it. First you have to clean it thoroughly. This can be done by leaving a solution of one tablespoon of trisodiumphosphate (TPS) and one gallon of water on the surface for twenty minutes. Be careful handling TPS because it can burn your skin—it's a good idea to wear long rubber gloves. This is also a great grout cleaner. Protect all your hard work by sealing the tile and grout. Apply sealer directly to the surface with a soft cloth. If you are only sealing the grout, apply directly on the grout lines using an artist's paintbrush. (I found mine in my kid's watercolor kit.) Wipe off any excess that lands on the tile. It's wise to do an additional coat immediately following the first.

Counter, Cabinet, and Sink Care

Countertops need daily attention: wipe up all crumbs with a soft cloth. Spray the surface with all-purpose cleanser. Weekly (and as needed): remove all items from the countertop. Dispose of crumbs, spray degreaser on any oil spots, and wipe away. Spray with disinfectant. Wipe down small appliances and the surface areas where they reside.

CLEANING CABINETS

Once a week, wipe down the drawer pulls and cabinets. Usually there are one or two heavy-use drawers that inevitably are opened with dirty hands during the cooking process. Don't let food crust onto the metals. Wipe clean and polish as needed. Once a month, wipe down the fronts of all your cabinets with an all-purpose cleaner and soft rag.

CLEANING AND MAINTAINING SINKS

It's best to get into the habit of rinsing the sink immediately so bits and pieces don't have a chance to dry onto the surface. A non-abrasive powder cleaner or a paste of baking soda and water works great for both stainless steel and porcelain sinks. Just sprinkle a tablespoon of baking soda in the sink and wipe with a damp sponge. Wet the sponge if you need more water. Rinse thoroughly to remove any residue. Use a nylon pad for tougher dirt.

On a weekly basis, scour and disinfect the sink. Grime accumulates around the base of the faucet, soap dispenser, and drain opening. Gently scrub these with soft toothbrush and a powder cleanser. Rinse or wipe away debris. Stainless steel sinks polish up with a bit of glass cleaner, all-purpose cleaner, vinegar, or ammonia. Wipe surfaces with a soft cloth to shine.

Porcelain sinks, especially white ones, will stain and scratch if care isn't taken to protect the surface. Use a rubber mat designed to protect the bottom. Stains can be buffed out with non-abrasive paste made with a quarter teaspoon of oxalic powder and a tablespoon of water. For a greener formula, try a sprinkle of cream of tartar and a teaspoon of hydrogen peroxide. Wait three minutes and scrub.

Avoiding Clogged Sinks

Get into the habit of preempting clogs by treating your sink on a weekly basis. Pour ¼ cup of baking soda followed by ½ cup of vinegar down the drain. Wait ten minutes and flush with water. If you have a garbage disposal, run some ice through it to clear any gunk that's accumulated.

Appliances

Your kitchen appliances are used often and come in direct contact with food. Therefore they need regular attention.

THE REFRIGERATOR

Cleaning out the refrigerator will keep it running better. Once a month, turn the temperature to Off and empty all the shelves and drawers. Throw out all outdated food. If you live in a warm climate, temporarily put all the perishable food in a cooler. Take the shelves and drawers out of the refrigerator and wash them with warm water and baking soda—one tablespoon to one cup of water. Let them air dry. Next, wipe out the interior walls and surfaces with a wet dish towel. Any crusty spills can be scrubbed off with a nylon pad and a paste of two teaspoons baking soda in one-quarter cup of water. The baking soda will go a long way toward dispelling odors. Don't forget to wipe off the rubber gasket around the door. Check for mildew and whether the seal is tight. Put all the food back in the refrigerator using the organizational method outlined in chapter 4. Next, wipe down the exterior sides and top of the refrigerator with a glass cleaner.

Now locate the refrigerator condenser coils. Most coils are situated at the bottom front and can be accessed by a removable grille. It's important to clean the dust off in order for the refrigerator to run efficiently. Don't freak out when you see all the dust! It's normal and has to be removed. A microfiber duster works well if you don't have a vacuum cleaner attachment that fits under the refrigerator.

Near the coils you'll find the drip pan. This catches the condensation that the refrigerator makes as it cools. Remove it carefully, dump the water, sanitize and replace.

Clean out the freezer every six months. Take everything out and put it in a cooler. Remove the shelves and wipe down the inside using the same method as for the refrigerator.

If water pools under the refrigerator, take the grille off the front and locate the drip pan. It might be overflowing or cracked. If it's not the drip pan, the ice maker line might be leaking. Pull the refrigerator away from the wall and unplug it. Locate the line running under the sink. If you see any leaks, use a wrench and try to tighten the connections. If the line itself is leaking, remove it and replace it.

Last, you may need to change the gasket, which is the rubber seal that keeps the door closed. Over time, it can mildew, warp, and crack. Order a new one from the manufacturer before you remove the old one! Also, remove the food from the door so that it's easier to work with. Soften the new gasket by soaking it in warm water. To remove the old gasket, loosen (not remove) the screws that hold it onto the door. They are under the seal. Pull out the old gasket. Replace it with the new one. Tighten the screws in the corners first, top and bottom next, and sides last. Check the door seal to make sure it's touching all the way around. If there is a gap, you need to take off the gasket and redo it.

SOLVING ICE MAKER PROBLEMS

Ice makers are the number one reason for service calls made on kitchen appliances. Here are a couple of things you can try to fix yourself.

If it's not making ice, check the temperature. It needs to be cold enough. Consult the temperature recommendations of the manufacturer.

If that's not it, the water line might be clogged. Pull the refrigerator out gently from the wall. Turn off the water supply valve located under the sink. Examine the water line for crimping. If it's bent, take an adjustable wrench and remove it. Replace with a new one. Don't forget to turn the water back on and check for leaks before you push the refrigerator back! Consider replacing it with a longer length for easy installation.

CLEARING A JAMMED GARBAGE DISPOSAL

If you hear a low hum instead of "crunch crunch," the garbage disposal has jammed. First, turn it off. Use a flashlight to determine whether debris is lodged next to the blades. After turning off the circuit breaker, use pliers to remove any particles you can see. If the motor is still jammed, locate the bottom of the garbage disposal under the sink. You'll see a hexagonal opening. This is where you insert the 6mm Allen wrench that came with the machine. Try to move it back and forth until the motor is freed. You can also try to free it by poking it with a long handle. If there is no power, push the little red button on the bottom to reset the disposal.

STOVETOP AND OVEN CARE

To keep your stove nice and shiny, wipe the surface every time you're done cooking. Porcelain and stainless steel clean up well with just a damp cloth. Soak burnt drippings with water for a few minutes and they should come up easily. A quick spray of a solution made of half vinegar and half water should peel off any leftover residue.

You can clean and polish on a weekly basis. This should incorporate a thorough cleaning of your cooktop and its elements. Certain radiant and solid cooktops require special polish, so follow the manufacturer's advice. Remove greasy drip pans and soak them in sudsy water or run them through the dishwasher. Lift up the top (if applicable) and wipe up crumbs. Wipe down grime from surrounding areas like the counter, backsplash, and control panel. Remove the electric elements to clean underneath them. Don't forget the grease filter under the exhaust fan. Remove the filter and soak it in water and ammonia.

The best way to minimize oven cleaning is to take care of spills immediately after they happen. Don't let a piece of cheese that dripped onto the bottom of the oven get baked into the surface repeatedly. One option is to spray a silicon-based product on the floor of a clean oven, which will make wiping easier. If a spill happens during cooking, sprinkle some table salt on it. It should wipe clean when the oven is cold. Some home cooks use aluminum foil to line the bottom of the oven. Check with the manufacturer to see if this is recommended and follow the directions. Another option is to place foods that drip, like pie or lasagna, on a piece of foil or a thin baking sheet before cooking.

There are three types of ovens, and their cleaning mechanisms require different care. A self-cleaning oven heats itself to a super-hot temperature that literally burns off all the food crusts. The best time to do this is at night while sleeping because the smells of the burning food can be unpleasant. Set the timer or turn it on before you go to bed. Two to three hours should work depending on how dirty the oven is.

A continuous-clean oven has a coated interior that oxidizes food spills each time you use it. It usually kicks in around 350 degrees. After a while, it too can have a buildup of spills that may require you to do a manual cleaning anyway.

If you have a conventional oven, use these tips to minimize the trauma of cleaning. Commercial oven cleaners smell bad and are expensive. Be prepared to open a window and put on gloves. It will ruin your floor, so protect the floor with newspapers in case anything drips. Some cleaners want you to preheat the oven before using, but check the directions on the can first because it may not be necessary. Also, you may need to extinguish the pilot light of a gas oven. Check your manufacturer's recommendations. Spray foam so it covers the dirty surfaces. This is the time to be frugal. Don't spray clean surfaces just to spray them. Also avoid the electrical elements and the light. Then get a roll of paper towels, nylon scrubber, and a candy bar (your treat when finished).

No matter what type of oven you have, don't leave the racks in the oven during the cleaning process because the finish will dull. If you want to clean the racks, place them in a large

Change the Light in Your Oven

Turn off the electricity or unplug the electric cord if it's a gas stove. Remove the glass guard surrounding the bulb by releasing the wire guide that holds it into place. Swap out the bulb for a new one with the same wattage. Replace the guard and wire guide.

garbage bag and spray with oven cleaner. Or place ½ cup of ammonia in the oven. Let them sit overnight. In the morning, wipe clean with paper towels and rinse. A mixture of ½ cup of vinegar and 1 gallon of water will get rid of any residue.

Another natural, inexpensive alternative to commercial oven cleaner is ammonia. But beware, ammonia can ruin some metal finishes. Go with what the manufacturer recommends. If you get the green light, place a bowl of full strength ammonia in the oven and leave it overnight. It will dissolve grease and films. Wipe out the loosened grime with paper towels and a nylon pad. Rinse with water and wipe dry.

Adjusting the Oven's Temperature

Oven temperatures need to be recalibrated every so often. If you have an oven with digital readouts, it's run by a computer and must be fixed by an authorized service person. If the oven has a temperature dial, remove the dial by pulling it straight off. The temperature adjustment dial is either on the back of the dial or on the face of the oven hidden by the dial. Find the screw that loosens a disk with series of notches. Depending on the oven, rotating the disk one notch clockwise or counterclockwise will lower or raise the temp 10 degrees. Replace the dial and test again.

MICROWAVE OVEN

Wipe up any crumbs or liquid spills with a wet cloth after each use. Then, once a week, clean and disinfect. Put a cup of water in the microwave on high for 1 minute. Let the steam it creates loosen any baked-on stains. Remove the turntable and clean in hot, soapy water. Scrub crusty dirt with a nylon pad and wipe down the insides with a damp cloth. Leave the door ajar to dry. Don't use any commercial cleaners.

TOASTER OVEN

Before initial use, unplug and turn it over. Open the bottom and line with aluminum foil. Line the removable tray with foil too. Throw away both pieces of foil after each oven use to keep bugs away. Wipe down the exterior with a damp cloth. Once a month, remove the wire racks and scour them in the sink. Remove the foil from the bottom and wipe out additional crumbs. Polish the exterior according to its material.

BLENDERS, CHOPPERS, AND FOOD PROCESSORS

After each use, disinfect and clean. Don't put plastic parts in the dishwasher because they can warp. Clean them with dish soap and warm water. Blenders can be filled with water and a dab of soap and run for a couple of minutes (with the top on!). Rinse with water and air-dry. Wipe the exteriors of all bases and polish them as needed. Scrape off food bits with a nylon scrubber.

COFFEEMAKER

Rinse the carafe clean after each use. To reduce scale and buildup, only use filtered water. To clean, wipe down the exterior with vinegar and water spray. Be careful not to wet the mechanical elements of the machine. Every three to six months you need to descale. Run a full pot of water with a cup of vinegar through a clean paper filter without any coffee. Discard the water. Run the complete cycle again with plain water.

DISHWASHER

Finally, an appliance that by virtue of its design appears to stay clean! But not so fast: debris can lodge on the inside, the seal can mildew, and minerals can cloud the interior. If you use the rinse cycle frequently, check for food particles and remove. It's also wise to examine the bottom and look for small items (usually sippy cup stoppers) that may have dropped near the heating elements. Wipe up the sides with a wet cloth and some baking soda. To deodorize, fill both detergent compartments with baking soda and run as normal.

Be careful running certain metals like aluminum or pewter through the dishwasher's drying cycle: the metal can discolor. Also, make sure to use a rinse aid. It helps prevent spotting during the drying cycle.

■Polishing Silver

Silver polish and a small cloth can do the trick, but it can take a long time and be exhausting. An alternative method involves a chemical reaction between washing soda and aluminum. Put some aluminum foil in the bottom of the sink. Dissolve 1 tablespoon of washing soda and fill 3 inches with hot water. Place silver items touching the aluminum foil. Watch the tarnish disappear. If the items look dull, a quick polish will finish the job.

GARBAGE CAN

Before you put in a new trash bag, place a clothes dryer softener sheet in the bottom of the trash can. It will keep it smelling nice. Once a week, rinse out the insides and wipe down the outside. If you have a faucet with a hose, you can try this in the kitchen, but you may want to take it outside and let it air dry.

7

Shopping for and Storing Fresh Food

Now that your *kitchen is functional and clean, it's time to start thinking about what you'll be doing in it. Hopefully, you're looking forward to cooking lots of delicious and healthy meals for your family. In order to do so, you need to know the ins and outs of buying the raw ingredients including the best places to find them, how to choose them, and how to keep your purchases as fresh as possible.*

In our modern era of food production and distribution, shopping for fresh food seems like a snap:

Get in car
Drive to store
Load cart
Pay
Drive home

But let's back up to the supermarket aisles, where the typical food choices are made. You can buy prepared meals (fresh or frozen), make some elements of each meal and buy others ready-made (bagged salads, frozen veggie mixes), or you can do everything from scratch. Each option has its own merits.

Prepackaged sanitized meals sit in our kitchens waiting to be opened, promising healthy, fresh dinners in minutes. Although there are some excellent prepackaged foods on the market today, most rarely deliver as promised. "Home-style" canned soups often have a chemical taste that lingers on your tongue. Frozen meals list so many ingredients that they sound like science experiments gone crazy—some of the stuff listed shouldn't even be called food. I believe that food costs are high enough you should think twice before giving away your money to big companies that make mediocre food with too much fat, sodium, and additives.

So, enough with the artificial stuff. Instead, fill up your cart with the best-looking produce, meat, and dairy products that you can afford. What better way to pay homage to your new kitchen life! Here's some concise information that will guide you through the fresh food maze.

Preparing for the Trip

There are two mistakes people make when shopping that end up costing them lots of money: impulse and overbuying. Making a list of things you need is therefore essential! It will curb impulsive spending and keep costs down, leaving you with more money in your pocket and less to worry about when you are trying to store your excess purchases later.

When you make your grocery list, draw a grid on a piece of paper. In each square, write down a heading that groups your groceries. Jot down ingredients that can be found together when shopping. For example, milk, cheeses, liquid non-dairy creamers, eggs, yogurt, etc. are usually grouped together in the refrigerated section. After a couple of trips, you can refine the list to reflect how the grocery store that you visit most often is set up.

It's nice to buy one or two items for everyone in the family. The night before shopping, ask other family members if they have any food suggestions. Kids love to be included in any decision-making process, and they can be a great help developing a wish list for snacks, lunches, and cereals they might want. Make sure it's called a "wish" list because every kid knows you don't get everything you wish for.

Next, go through the recipes you intend to make and write down all the ingredients you need to buy in the grid, coded so that you remember which ingredients go with which recipes. There's nothing worse than assuming that an ingredient is actually in your pantry. If you have multiple chefs or use things up regularly, it's impossible to remember what you have. If you're very organized, or have read chapter 4, you've already created your pantry supply list located at the door or on the back of a cabinet.

Don't be overly ambitious in trying to make too many things in a week. You'll end up with an overstuffed refrigerator, throwing out unused spoiled vegetables, and throwing up your hands in despair. Know your family's schedule and plan accordingly. A sensible approach is to look at the calendar and plan for the nights you actually can cook, which nights no one will be home to eat, and which night you want a break. For instance, two dinners from scratch, two easy-to-make-ahead dinners, one night out, one night of pizza, and one night of leftovers.

Lastly, prepare the trunk of your car to make room for the groceries. Consider keeping a small cooler in the trunk. Everyone likes to combine errands so don't take the chance of letting your ice cream melt. Perishable items will probably keep long enough for one or two stops. Also, buy some collapsible crates to hold those flimsy grocery bags. These can make transferring shopping bags to the house much more efficient, and they don't take much storage room.

Clip and Snip for Savings

Clipping coupons can save you money, but only if you know how to maximize them. Go through the coupons from your weekly newspaper or supermarket circular before you shop. If you use certain products regularly, visit the manufacturers' Web sites to find out about downloadable coupons and easy-to-use recipes that can be emailed to you. Local stores often put items on sale to coincide with manufacturers' weekly coupons. Take advantage of this strategy and stock up, but only on the sale items that your family frequently uses.

KNOW THE GROWING SEASONS

As consumers demand more products out of season, it's getting harder to know when something is "in season." Grapes in the middle of winter? No problem! Spring onions in the fall, why not? In a global economy, the choices of available food are really remarkable. Since everybody can get just about anything at any time, the average person doesn't know a growing season from a persimmon.

Here's a hint. When something seems really expensive, it's usually an indication that the traditional growing season is over. Getting to know the growing seasons can provide you with a new appreciation for the variable quality of produce and what to expect for your money. The growing season in both the northern and southern hemisphere is from the last day of frost until the first day of frost. Temperate climates, located closer to the equator, can grow crops all year round. Pick your produce and plan your menus around what is in season (**7.1**).

▶ **7.1** Get to know what fruits and vegetables are in season at any particular time.

■Seasonal Buying Guide

Early spring: Asparagus, artichokes, baby onions, rhubarb, endive, leeks, strawberries, pears, plums.

Late spring— early summer: Apricots, cantaloupes, cherries, rhubarb, plums, peas.

Summer: Peaches, nectarines, figs, raspberries, blueberries, plums, watermelon, beets, corn, okra, peas, tomatoes.

Fall: Apples, cranberries, broccoli, cauliflower, corn, sweet potatoes.

Late fall—winter: Apples, pears, grapefruit, oranges, lemons, limes, Brussels sprouts, endive, leeks.

SPECIALTY INGREDIENTS

The obvious draw to a supermarket is getting everything you need in one stop. But they can't carry everything that might please your family's unique tastes and interests. If you enjoy cooking and eating certain regional or ethnic foods, you'll find a trip to an ethnic grocery store an exciting and educational experience. Usually owned by first- or second-generation immigrants, the items stocked are imported directly from the country of origin. The owners can guide you through the maze of products so that you can get exactly what you need. For instance, you'll be surprised just how many types of soy sauce there are, or find wonderfully packaged Japanese treats that you can stick in lunch boxes.

A lot of the time, the ethnic foods that your regular grocery store stocks will be more expensive than those found at the specialty shop. For example, jasmine rice purchased from an ethnic grocer can be had for a fraction of the price than if bought at a regular supermarket. In this case, the smaller shopkeeper can order direct and in bulk because he knows that his customers will always buy it. If you don't have access to local specialty food stores, you can always try the food stores in cyberspace. The Internet is a great place to get ideas for cooking new things. Specialty ingredients can easily be shipped to you in quantities that make it attractive to explore.

TOP FOOD SHOPPING TIPS

Your adventure begins when you arrive at the store. So many brands, so many choices. Here's a quick list of ideas to help you fill your basket and get out of the store and back into your kitchen.

1. If you like to try new things, purchase the new product but also buy the one you usually get. That way if the new one just doesn't taste the way you want it, you'll still have something to work with.

2. Check the date. Most products, even dry goods, have a shelf life. Some are days, some are weeks. If you find a product that's expired, notify a stock person. They most likely will be happy to get you a fresh one and dispose of the out-of-date product.

3. Shop at a busy market. The turnover of supply is faster at a busy market. The more shoppers to buy the groceries, the faster the store has to restock, hence the food is delivered more frequently and you benefit.

4. Find out when certain items are delivered during the course of a week. The next time you're in the grocery store, ask the various managers (deli, produce, and dairy) exactly when they receive their deliveries. Chances are it's two or three times a week on very specific days. Plan your shopping around that. You'll be sure that you're getting the freshest food. Allow enough time for the product to get onto the shelves.

5. Can't find it? Ask for it! If you can't find a new product you've heard about, ask the manager to order it for you. Most local grocery stores want to help you as much as possible. Why? They want your business. You're providing valuable feedback about what customers really want. When I was pregnant, I craved an old-fashioned salad dressing that I hadn't seen in years. The manager was able to get a case of it, and it was there for me the next week. Other people must have been happy to see it because it's been at the store ever since!

6. Pick your produce from the back of the shelf. Shops usually put the stock that is expiring up front, in hopes of selling it first.

7. Don't buy anything near the cashier. These are "impulse buys" and the prices are often jacked up.

8. Don't be fooled by half-price specials. Many times the product offered is the worst deal in terms of price per ounce.

9. Check your receipts, even after you get home. Any mistakes will be rectified to your satisfaction because the store wants to retain its customers.

10. Choose paper bags over plastic, but only if they have handles. You can recycle these when you get home, or reuse them for a multitude of projects.

Besides ethnic stores, specialty shops that focus on one type of food are always a treat. Cheese shops, a fishmonger, or a vegetable stand can provide more, and fresher, varieties than a chain supermarket. In addition, the staff will be able to spend time helping you with your purchases, making you a more educated consumer. Plus, you'll be shopping locally instead of "nationally," which directly benefits your town's economy.

ALTERNATIVE LOCAL SUPPLIERS

The benefits of eating fresh-grown produce far outweigh the extra effort to obtain it. Fruits and vegetables that don't have to ripen on the truck just taste better and have many more nutrients. Farm co-ops can be a great way to reconnect with local food farms in your area. Most co-ops provide fresh produce weekly to customers during a set growing season. For a fee, you'll receive a selection of whatever is growing that week. Talk about fresh! If you are concerned about pesticides, inquire what type of farming they practice.

Farmers markets are another option. Usually they begin in late spring and end in early fall, depending on the weather. Some warm weather areas have farmers markets all year round. In addition to produce, farmers markets showcase local food producers' homemade products not available in stores. You can find specialty cheeses, homemade salsa and jellies, cakes and cookies, locally farmed honey, plants, flowers, bulk nuts, pestos, and pasta sauces. It's a great way to support small local businesses.

Some flea markets also have onsite produce that's usually well priced, but shop early in the morning. Produce that has been sitting around outside all day is just not going to hold up as well as refrigerated produce.

ORGANIC VS. CONVENTIONALLY GROWN PRODUCE

The controversy of organic vs. conventional farming methods has raged for years. Chemical pesticides were introduced to modern farming about fifty years ago. In order to boost food production, farmers needed to respond to the low yield and potentially catastrophic results that occur due to pest infestation. Most of the developed nations in the world have government agencies that oversee the application of pesticides and adherence to guidelines promoting the safest way to use them. The farming industry is highly regulated to ensure compliance in this very important area. Whether compliance is achieved remains a question. There's just no way to know if that apple you bought yesterday was properly sprayed or not. Our bodies are designed to rid ourselves of toxins, so the small amount of residue found on your morning strawberries is probably not enough to be toxic. But given the chemicals needed to produce everything from bedding to hairspray, an overload of toxins is possible. Small children, who are still developing their central nervous systems, brains, and other organs, are at the greatest risk for overexposure to pesticides.

But that's not all. According to the World Health Organization, too many developing countries lack any method, much less plan, to implement, control, or regulate farming practices. This is a big red light! Remember the upside of our global marketplace, and the year-round availability of grapes? These go hand in hand. The amount of imported fruits and vegetables is increasing every year.

As of now, there are many persuasive arguments for and against buying organically. Organic farming has taken off as a result of concerns regarding these matters. Organic farmers have to adhere to a set of rigorous and strictly enforced guidelines forbidding the use of synthetic pesticides and fertilizers, antibiotics, artificial ingredients, genetically modified products, irradiation, and sewage sludge in order to receive an FDA seal of approval. Studies have shown organic produce may also contain more vitamins and minerals than conventionally grown foods, specifically, higher amounts of antioxidants and omega fatty acids in dairy products, eggs, and fruits. But these findings of higher vitamin and mineral content could very well be more about handling, processing, and storage practices rather than the actual farming method. Organic products are typically more expensive and not readily available. Sometimes the produce is superior in taste and quality, but sometimes it's inferior and inedible.

■Conventionally Grown Foods with the Highest Amount of Pesticides

1. Apples	6. Cherries
2. Apricots	7. Green beans
3. Bell peppers	8. Peaches
4. Cantaloupe	9. Spinach
5. Celery	10. Strawberries

BUT WAIT, THERE'S MORE TO WORRY ABOUT

Food contaminated by harmful bacteria is more of a threat to your health than pesticides. For years, various reported outbreaks of disease-causing microbes have been found in our food supply. Sickness and occasional death can be traced to e. coli, salmonella (from exposure to raw chicken), "Mad Cow" disease, shigella, and cyclospora.

The good news is that there are now ways to reduce your exposure to all these threats. Cautious food handling should be practiced at all times. It takes a bit more of your time, but it's critical. Adhere to the following safety practices to protect yourself and your family.

Choosing and Storing Produce

Throwing out the produce you bought just two days ago is more than a little frustrating. Knowing how to pick the freshest fruit and vegetables possible and the best way to store them goes a long way toward minimizing aggravation and maximizing what's in your wallet. First, always look for unbruised fruit and vegetables with no visible brown spots. Avoid any produce that has mold on it, wilting greens attached, cuts or nicks that expose the insides, and wrinkled or shriveled skin. Whatever you need to use immediately, purchase ripe. For later in the week, choose fruits that need to ripen further.

TOP FOOD HANDLING TIPS

1. Wash hands before touching any raw food.

2. Washing your produce with warm soapy water can eliminate a host of chemicals and potentially harmful bacteria. Removing a fruit or vegetable's outer skin completely and discarding the outer leaves of leafy vegetables is even more effective.

3. Wash prepackaged produce even though it says "rinsed and ready to use." E. coli bacteria has been found on these types of products.

4. Zap cold cuts in the microwave for 20 seconds on high or until steaming hot to kill listeria, a deadly bacteria.

5. Rinse meat and fish in cold running water and pat dry with a clean paper towel before cooking.

6. Use separate cutting boards for vegetables, meat, seafood, and fruit.

7. Serve cooked meat on a clean plate, not on the one you used before cooking.

8. Never reuse a marinade as a basting sauce.

9. Clean and then disinfect your sinks and countertops frequently.

10. Use a meat thermometer to determine when meat is fully cooked. Follow these suggested guidelines:

    Cooked ham 130°F/43°C

    Beef (rare) 140°F/60°C

    Beef (med), smoked ham 160°F/71°C

    Pork, veal, beef (well) 170°F/76°C

    Lamb 180°F/80°C

    Poultry 185°F/85°C

Most fruits and vegetables last longer in a cool, moist environment. The drawers in the bottom of the refrigerator are designed to keep out the dry air that is recirculated from the freezer. If you have an adjustable temperature or humidity drawer, it should do the job nicely.

Unripened fruit must be left out on the counter until ripe. This would include bananas, peaches, plums, pears, tomatoes, cantaloupe, and honeydew. Place them in a paper bag and then crumple up the top. Leave the bag in a sunny spot in your kitchen. In a day, you'll notice a remarkable difference.

All fruits and vegetables begin to deteriorate after being picked, some simply faster than others. Only wash produce right before you use it since it will stay fresher. Fruit that should be stored unwashed in the refrigerator includes citrus and berries, apples, grapes, and ripe melons.

Some fruits, like bananas, will turn black and look less appealing as the week goes on. Actually, bananas should only be eaten once this darkening occurs: a clear yellow skin shows that the fruit is not completely ripe. Other fruits turn brown or black once their flesh has been exposed to air. This is called oxidation. Avocados, apples, or pears are good examples. To store after cutting, tightly press plastic wrap to any exposed insides. This will slow down the oxidation process.

Most vegetables can be stored unwashed in the vegetable bin of your refrigerator. If your veggies are rotting at record pace, you may need to check the temperature of the bin. The temperature should be between 35–40 degrees. Fresh vegetables should last 2–4 days so it's best to buy what you are going to use not too far in advance. Usually the weekly shopping trip can be augmented with a mid-week stop for more milk and fresh produce.

Some veggies like potatoes, sweet potatoes, and winter squashes last longer when stored at higher temperatures. Potatoes do best at 40 degrees. Sweet potatoes and squashes like it higher at 55–60 degrees. Believe it or not, the ideal place to store these foods would be in the refrigerator door. It's always the warmest spot! Buy an open plastic container that fits in the lower bin of your door and put them in there.

Lettuce is a delicate vegetable that is highly susceptible to higher temperatures. Right after you buy it, put it in a zip storage bag and place it in a cold vegetable bin. When you want to use it, soak it in a clean sink full of water and rub dirt off the leaves. Pat dry with paper towels or use a salad spinner. Don't cut leaves with a knife because the edges turn brown. Gently tear with your hands. If you have leftovers, wrap the leaves in paper towel and put them in a plastic zipper bag. The paper towels will absorb the excess water as well as keep the lettuce crisp and fresh for three or four more days.

Most cooks will tell you that there is no substitute for using fresh herbs in a recipe (**7.2**). However, herbs wilt at an alarming rate so purchase what you need when you need it. There are two ways to store them. Either method should preserve fresh herbs for about a week.

The first method is to cut off the ends of the stems, like you would fresh flowers. Wrap the ends in a damp paper towel and place in a zipped bag. Check daily and snip and change the paper towel when the herbs start to droop. The second method is to snip the stems and place upright in a plastic cup with an inch of water, carefully keeping any leaves out of the water. Store in the refrigerator for up to two weeks. Change the water every other day.

Fresh herbs can also be frozen but they will lose their bright green appearance and turn dark. When this happens, chop them up and place in ice cube trays with a tiny amount of water. Store the frozen cubes in a zipper bag and use individually for flavoring soups or sauces.

▲ **7.2** Fresh herbs, like rosemary, add zing to any recipe.

■Freezing Fruits and Vegetables

A visit to a local farm can provide hours of fun for the entire family, especially if you can pick your own strawberries, raspberries, or blueberries. You can eat to your heart's content there, but have a plan to keep the extras you bring home. Freezing berries is easy. First, rinse them well, and then place them individually on cookie sheets, allowing them to dry completely. You can speed up the process by blow drying them at a cool setting. Then, place them in a plastic zipper storage bag and freeze until you are ready to use them. When you need them, place the whole bag in the fridge for an hour and they will be just as good as the day you picked them. Husk corn and peel peaches before freezing.

Choosing Meats

Fresh meat has a limited shelf life so it needs to be kept in very cold refrigeration. Most supermarkets purchase larger pieces of meat or whole chickens. They then cut them into various parts and pre-pack them with a "sell by" date. When you make your purchase, be sure the date hasn't expired. Sometimes, meat about to expire will be marked down so think twice about buying it to stock for the freezer. It's best to use it immediately.

Raw meat has a distinct odor. However, it shouldn't be a strong sour or foul smell. Look for meat that is moist and tender to the touch, not mushy. Color is not a good indication of freshness because oxidation will turn meat different colors even if it's still good. Look for some marbling—the white streaks of fat that run through the muscle. This will melt as you cook it and makes for a tender cut. Go for boneless steaks rather than those with bones if you want more meat for your money!

Lastly, there are fast-cooking meats and those intended for slow cooking. The longer-cooking meats, called roasts, butts, or rounds, need to be cooked for a greater time to become tender. If you've never bought one, don't be intimidated by the size! Once you cook a roast, you'll realize how easy it is. Leftovers make great sandwiches.

Beef is graded according to how marbled it is. Most likely, you will have a hard time getting your hands on the best pieces because they are usually sold to restaurants and hotels. Independent butchers, either in their local stores or on the Internet, will sell those more expensive cuts of meat, and will be able to prepare it for cooking to your exact specifications.

The most expensive cuts of beef, pork, and other game animals (like deer or elk) are the naturally tender rib and loin sections. These are passive muscle areas. The parts that move around the most—the shoulder, flank, and leg—tend to be tougher. They will require more preparation and cooking to make the meat tender enough to eat. Ground beef is the least expensive meat and a very popular product. Unfortunately, it's made of the lowest grade beef available and the extra processing makes it more susceptible to airborne pathogens and bacterial contamination. Ground sirloin is a better choice, especially if you are also interested in counting fat grams. If the supermarket or local butcher can't prepare this for you, you can buy sirloin and grind it yourself with the food grinder attachment on a standing mixer.

Storing Meat Purchases

Meat needs to be cooked immediately, marinated for a future meal, or frozen. You can freeze meats that will be used in less than a month in the store's wrap. For bulk purchases or meat that won't be used quickly, repackage it yourself in freezer paper and zipper bags as described below. The key is to eliminate any air or vapors from reaching the surface of the meat. If you know that you plan on storing meat for one to two months, have the butcher shrink-wrap it for you.

Using freezer paper: Measure a piece of freezer paper as if you were wrapping a gift, then add 6–8 more inches. Place meat in the center of the paper. If you are freezing more than one piece, place a piece of wax paper between each piece. Grab the paper and match up both ends above the meat. Press them together and fold in one direction down toward the meat, pressing the air out as you go. Fold the sides up and secure with paper tape. Write the item, weight or amount of pieces, and date of purchase on the paper. Place the paper in a freezer-weight zipper bag for extra protection (**7.3**). The same holds true for bulk purchases of poultry or pork. Hamburgers and meatballs can be pre-formed and frozen for a future meal. Place meatballs or patties on a cookie sheet until frozen, then store in a freezer bag stacked and wrapped in freezer paper.

Marinating, then freezing meat: If you want to be a step ahead, you can marinate meat and freeze it for a future meal. Prepare the marinade, place washed meat in a zipper plastic bag, and pour marinade over it. Squeeze out any extra air from the bag and zip. Plan to use within a week or two because the marinade may change the texture of the meat.

Defrosting: Always defrost meat in the refrigerator. Slow thawing will keep the meat moister and won't allow bacteria to grow. Place the frozen meat in a glass dish to catch any juices from leaking onto the shelf. Larger cuts or whole birds, like turkey, may require you to defrost one or two days ahead. You can also defrost meat in a microwave oven, but you will often run the risk of the microwave actually cooking the meat. Follow directions for the power setting and time exactly in order to avoid this common problem.

▲ **7.3** Store meat in freezer paper, label it, and place your wrapped items in a zipper lock plastic bag for extra protection.

◼The Deli Counter

If you're stuck for new lunch ideas, check out some of the gourmet meats and sandwich stuffers that are now offered at the deli counter. Everyone loves a fresh deli sandwich. BBQ chicken, rosemary turkey breast, and Cajun ham are some interesting choices. To be safe, buy your deli products from a store where the employees are required to use plastic gloves. Only buy what you think you'll use for 3–5 days. Deli meats can be frozen for 1–2 months, but sliced meats don't freeze as well due to moisture absorption.

Cheeses from the deli can be purchased sliced or by the quarter pound. They'll keep about a month if you buy a large chunk and slice it yourself. Keep the cheese tightly wrapped in plastic so the odors are contained and the edges don't harden.

CURED AND SMOKED MEATS

Sausages and bacon can add a delicious twist to a home-cooked meal, whether it is breakfast, lunch, or dinner. They can be sautéed or grilled and then added to soups or eaten as a sandwich, making them extremely versatile.

Sausage varieties usually reflect regional cuisine. Flavors vary widely, so look at the spices listed on the label. Some are spicy, some are sweet. Don't be afraid to experiment with new brands. Store sausages in their original container in the freezer or refrigerator.

Bacon is another item that can be purchased either prepackaged or by the pound from the butcher's counter. Fresh bacon can be smoked with various woods that will impart subtle flavors. It should also be left in its store packaging, refrigerated or frozen.

If you only plan to use a slice at a time, here's a storage trick. Separate the bacon strips and lay them out on a piece of freezer paper, with a 2" inch space in between. Roll up like a jelly roll and store in a freezer zip bag. As you need it, unroll and peel off a frozen strip.

Choosing and Storing Fish

The freshest choices of fish are either "fresh" or "flash frozen" (meaning fish that is frozen on the boat, and not in a factory). There is usually no discernable difference in the taste. Plan on eating the fish you buy the same night, or freezing it for the future. When picking out a whole fish, look for shiny eyes, no fishy smell, and smooth scales. If you are purchasing fillets, ask when the fish was cut. The more recent, the better. A fillet should not have any dryness to it, nor browning or yellowing of the edges. If you see fresh blood, that's a good sign, not bad. Transport your fish home in a cooler that you brought with a take-along ice pack. Or have the fishmonger double-bag your fish with ice, and then bag that twice at the checkout for the trip home.

Storing Dairy Products

Milk, cheese, butter, and cultured milk products make up the dairy section. Cultured dairy products include sour cream, cottage cheese, cream cheese, and yogurt. Eggs are thrown into the dairy section because, aside from needing to be refrigerated, back in the old days they were delivered by the milkman. Eggs keep for three to four weeks. A fresh egg floats on water, in case you're interested in testing it. Always store the eggs in a container because the shells are porous and they pick up odors.

All dairy products need constant refrigeration to maintain freshness. Take note of the "best if used by" or expiration dates on them. Look for the container with the furthest future expiration date on it: that's the one to buy. Butter keeps well but is susceptible to oxidation. Always rewrap butter in plastic wrap so that none of it is left out in the open. Store extra sticks of butter in the freezer for up to three months. Cultured soft cheese products, like feta and fresh mozzarella, need to be used within a few days. To keep them fresher, change the water they are soaking in daily. Never eat cheese or yogurt products that have mold on them.

Hard cheeses keep for a long time in plastic wrap: up to three months opened, six months unopened. Instead of buying the ready-made parmesan in a can, keep a hunk of real parmesan in the refrigerator and bring it to the table to grate like they do in an Italian restaurant. Kids really love it when you grate it in a dramatic fashion.

Buying and Storing Bread

Breads are sold in a variety of ways. Pre-sliced, pre-packed bread is delivered frequently to stores, so freshness isn't often an issue, but, once again, checking the "best if used by" date won't hurt. Bread sold from the bakery section is baked daily, unless otherwise marked. Day-old bread can be had for a discount, which would be fine for making croutons or bread pudding.

Store bread at room temperature or freeze it. Freezing bread is easy and keeps it the freshest. Save one section of your freezer for all your breads and it's easy to keep track of what you have. Beware of freezer burn, which tends to affect bread pretty badly. Always place the bread in a freezer zipper bag for extra protection.

Slice all your bread before you freeze it. A whole loaf can be frozen wrapped in aluminum foil, then placed in a zipper freezer bag. Pre-sliced bread should be double-bagged as well. Frozen, pre-sliced bagels, English muffins, and sandwich breads can go straight to the toaster, no need to defrost them.

Purchasing and Storing Chocolate

Buying chocolate for cooking is a lot like choosing a wine. The basic style might be outlined in the recipe, but after that you're on your own. Each chocolate company uses different sources of cocoa, different ingredients, and even different techniques for making their product. The end result is a huge range of flavors, textures, and aromas. The best way to pick chocolate is to taste it yourself. Even though there are guidelines for buying chocolate, ultimately, your taste buds will lead you to the right brand to buy. First, it shouldn't have any bitter aftertaste. It should also be uniform in color. White or gray streaks indicate it's past its "bloom."

Chocolate falls in two categories: sweetened and unsweetened. Sweetened chocolate is chocolate liquor with a sweetener. Depending on the percentage of chocolate liquor, it's called either bittersweet, semi-sweet or sweetened. The best dark chocolate has at least 70 percent cacao. Unsweetened chocolate is 100 percent chocolate liquor. This is preferred by most bakers

▲ **7.4** There are many types of chocolate; most bakers prefer to use unsweetened dark chocolate.

because it allows them to control the amount of sweetness in the dessert (**7.4**). Make sure not to substitute sweetened for unsweetened because the recipe has been already adjusted to allow for the difference in sugar. White chocolate isn't really chocolate at all. It's just the cocoa butter, sugar, milk solids, and added flavors. As a rule, the higher the percentage of cocoa butter, the better tasting it will be (and more expensive!).

You can store chocolate in a cool, dark area in 60-70 degrees and less than 50 percent humidity. It can be stored for up to a year.

Buying Coffee

Coffee is a simple pleasure in many people's lives. Next time you visit your local coffee shop, ask some questions about the coffee. Many coffee shops roast their own beans, giving them a unique flavor that can't be replicated (**7.5**). The quality and freshness is also unbeatable. Coffee beans come from either the Arabica or Robusta coffee tree. Arabica coffee is hard to grow and produces a smaller harvest. It produces a superior coffee and is more expensive than Robusta.

▲ **7.5** Locally roasted beans provide unique, fresh flavor.

If you taste a cup of coffee that you love, find out what type of bean is being used. Also find out where it's from. Different countries produce different beans, all with their own unique tastes. You may have seen coffee marketed as Fair-trade coffee. Fair-trade coffee is purchased directly from growers cutting out the traditional middlemen that take advantage of local farmers. Fair-trade coffee promotes shade grown crops and sustainable agricultural practices.

Next determine how the coffee was roasted. Lighter roasts produce sweeter coffee beans that allow the original flavors to come through better. Darker roasts produce a stronger, less acidic coffee bean. For home use, there are three simple rules for making great coffee: Buy it often, buy it fresh, and grind it daily. Coffee starts to deteriorate the second it's ground. Purchase your coffee in whole bean form and grind it at home or at the supermarket grinder. It just takes a few more seconds in the process and the benefits are great. Store it in an airtight container. Follow the instructions with your coffeemaker and adjust the grind accordingly.

8 Stocking a Pantry

If the kitchen *is the heart of your home, the pantry is the blood that keeps it running. Having a well-stocked pantry will making cooking easier and more fun. First, a good cook needs to have the right ingredients on hand. Running to the store for every recipe takes its toll. I'm sure that there's probably a core group of foods that you and your family use most frequently. Keeping a list of these items and tracking their consumption will eliminate running out of these very important staples!*

If you have picky eaters in your household, backups are a must. When my son was three, he was on the "beige" diet, as we called it. He would only eat food that was white: plain pasta, mashed potatoes, rice. You get the picture. As you can imagine, our pantry was fully stocked with these items. After all, these were the staples of my menu planning for at least a year.

Use this chapter as a guide to keep your dry goods well stocked so you can prepare almost any recipe with ease. If you're interested in expanding your pantry to include some foods that you may not have tried before, mini-descriptions should help you with your picks. Once you've stocked your pantry, you are well on your way toward maintaining sanity in the kitchen!

The Perfect Pantry

A well-stocked pantry includes:

▶ Ingredients that are fresh and ready to use, not three years old and suspicious looking.
▶ The ability to substitute other ingredients when you are in a pinch.
▶ All your family favorites.
▶ Organization that makes it easy to create a shopping list.

Pantry Placement

Pantry items include everything that can sit on a shelf without needing refrigeration. In an organized pantry, foods are grouped into categories that make finding what you need fast and easy (**8.1**). Larger items should be stored behind smaller items. Heavier items, like bags of rice, should be stored at waist level so that you don't strain your back to pick them up. Items that are frequently used need to be accessible. Place all labels facing out so that you can immediately see what you have. If there are duplicates, place the second item behind the first. Light, larger items, like cereal boxes, crackers, and pasta can go higher up. If you want the kids to get their own cereal, place it on a shelf they can reach. Consider creating a snack shelf that they are allowed to access themselves without mishap.

▲ 8.1 An organized pantry makes your kitchen more manageable.

■Storing Dry Goods

Stocking a variety of pasta, beans, and grains gives you many options for cooking healthy, fast meals. Storing dry goods properly will ensure that the products stay as fresh as possible and limit the pests that can accompany them into your house. Once opened, everything should be stored in either plastic bags or containers. And make sure that they are well-labeled with date of purchase!

Inventory 101

A well-stocked pantry has what are called "food staples," which are the basic canned goods, sauces, and condiments that most people use. Some people go through ketchup like water, so having one or two extra bottles on hand is a good idea. Other people make black bean soup or nachos every week, so they need to stock up on the ingredients required for those recipes. Someone who bakes all the time has more baking ingredients than someone who doesn't.

However, there are a core group of foods that most people stock. Keep in mind that there are so many different things to buy in each category that personal preference should win out every time. Don't feel like you have to buy something just to have it, unless you like experimenting. If so, and if you have the space, every item on these lists can be a must-have for you.

PASTA

Pasta comes in hundreds of different shapes and sizes (**8.2**). Smaller shapes are perfect for soups and salads. Long, thick ribbons are good for baked casseroles. Skinny rods like spaghetti or linguini are made to be served with smooth, runny sauces. Shorter, thicker shapes like penne or rotini work best with chunky sauces. Make sure to have a good variety in the pantry at all times. Traditional pasta is made of durum wheat, but Asian noodles are also made from rice flour. Dry pasta has a shelf life of six months to a year.

For smooth sauces, choose rods:

Angel hair: The thinnest strand.

Capellini: A bit thicker than angel hair.

Spaghetti: Long thin strands.

Vermicelli: Thicker strands than capellini.

For thicker, creamier sauces, choose ribbons:

Fettuccini: Long, thin ribbons.

Lasagna: Long, very wide ribbons.

Linguini: Long, thin ribbons, thinner than fettuccini.

Tagliatelle: Long, wide ribbons.

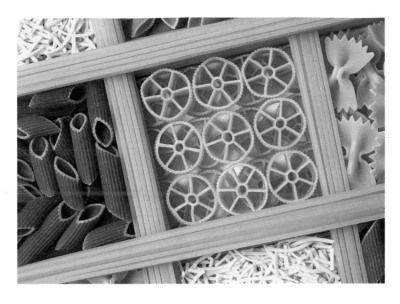

◀ 8.2 Pasta comes in many varieties to accommodate different types of sauces and moods.

For chunky sauces:

Cavatelli: Shaped liked little hotdog buns.

Farfalle: Shaped like bow ties.

Fusilli: Shaped like a corkscrew.

Orecchiette: Shaped like little saucers or "ears."

For soups or risotto:

Alphabets: Tiny letter-shaped pasta.

Elbow macaroni: Small bent tubes.

Orzo: Tiny barley-shaped pasta.

Tubettini: Small tubes.

For Asian noodle dishes:

Ramen noodles: Japanese wheat noodles fried in oil, then dried for use in soups.

Rice vermicelli: Thin strands of noodles made from rice with a cellophane consistency.

Soba noodles: Thinner noodles made from wheat and buckwheat, usually eaten cold with a dipping sauce.

Udon: Thick, wheat noodles used in Japanese soups and stir-fry.

BEANS

Beans are loaded with nutrients, fiber, and protein. They can be purchased in bulk and stored dry. To use in any recipe, dry beans require prep time. Beans have to be soaked, some of them overnight, before you can start cooking with them. Therefore, it's good to keep a variety of canned beans as well for emergencies, or for a quick meal during a busy week.

Black beans: Also known as turtle beans, they are a staple of Latin American cooking.

Cannelloni beans: Known also as white kidney beans, these are great in soups.

Chili beans: A smaller version of the pinto bean, also used in refried beans and chili.

Kidney beans: Deep brownish red beans used in hearty soups and chilies, as well as bean salad.

Navy beans: Commonly used in baked beans.

Pinto beans: Used in refried beans and chili.

GRAINS

How a grain is processed affects the amount of nutrients, the way it's cooked, and its taste. Whole grains, which are produced with the outer husk intact, are heavier, chewier, and take longer to cook. They are the healthiest for you and pack the most fiber but they can be difficult to digest. Pearled or polished grains have had this husk removed, and with it goes most of the nutrients. These are usually what most people like to eat, since they have a silkier feel and cook relatively quickly. If you are pressed for time but want to add nutrients, try some of the quick-cooking versions of grains that are pre-cooked and reduce preparation time. Avoid buying high-priced prepackaged grains with herbs and seasoning. Along with those seasonings come a host of artificial ingredients. You can easily make better tasting versions yourself at home.

Common flours made from grains:

Bread flour: A high-gluten wheat flour with barley flour and vitamin C added to increase the loft and chewiness. It's not advisable to substitute bread flour for cake flour.

Buckwheat flour: A nutty darker flour, often used in pancakes.

White flour/cake flour: A low-gluten, high-starch wheat flour that has been highly processed and usually bleached. Made from ground wheat kernels, it's used for baking when a lighter texture is desired.

Whole wheat flour: A heartier, darker, unbleached, wheat flour made from whole wheat grains. To boost fiber, substitute ⅓ to ½ of the whole wheat flour called for with white flour.

Commonly used for cereal, soups, and side dishes:

Barley: A chewy, nutty grain with high nutritional content. Prepared as a hot cereal or side dish, it is usually purchased pearled or unprocessed (also known as hulled).

Buckwheat groats: The inner kernel of the buckwheat grain stripped of its inedible outer skin. Usually crushed and toasted in oil to remove bitter flavor. Used as a side dish or hot cereal.

Bulgur: Wheat berries that have been cleaned, cracked, and cooked, making them faster to prepare. Similar to couscous in taste and texture. Used for making tabbouleh salad.

Corn grits: Corn that's been ground into a fine grain of sand, usually prepared as a side dish. Used for making polenta.

Couscous: Wheat that has been ground, steamed, and dried. Like rice, a popular side dish in many Middle Eastern cultures.

Millet: This grain is popular when a gluten-free diet is required. Mostly found in ready-made cereals. Toasting improves the flavor.

Quinoa: An ancient grain known in health food circles, quinoa virtually makes a complete protein by itself. It should be rinsed well and toasted before cooking. Its springy texture and light taste take on any flavor that is added to it.

Rice: The edible seed of a grass, a staple used for making cereal, bread, side dishes, flours, and beverages. Most common forms are long, medium, and short grain.

Spelt: An ancient form of wheat, you may substitute spelt for any whole wheat recipe and you'll get more vitamins, protein, and fiber in your dishes. Spelt is not as glutinous as whole wheat, so baking with it can be tricky. To minimize crumbling, make sure the batter or dough is mixed long enough.

CRACKERS

When stocking up on crackers, buy various flavors such as sesame, garlic, or cheese, as well as a variety of consistencies. Various thicknesses should be considered depending upon the heft of the topping. For hors d'oeuvres, purchase crackers that have good crunch and light taste. If you are dipping or scooping, get a cracker that won't fall apart and leave a wake of crumbs in the dip! Crackers made with hydrogenated vegetable oil have a better flake and crunch than all-natural crackers, but they aren't as healthy for you. Crackers will keep unopened for a couple months, but be sure to use them within a week once you open them.

Butter crackers: A soft, crumbly cracker that imparts a butter flavor. Use alone or with cut cheeses.

Cheese crackers: Crackers flavored with a combination of piquant spices and cheese.

Oyster crackers: Small salty crackers formed in hexagon shapes, often sprinkled in soups.

Rice crackers: A crisp, hard cracker made from rice flour.

Rye crackers: Crunchy, high fiber crackers used in place of bread for sandwiches.

Sesame crackers: Water crackers with sesame seeds on them, used for dips or spreads.

Water crackers: A neutral-flavored cracker that won't compete with a dip or spread.

CANNED FOODS FOR THE PANTRY

Studies show that canned, fresh, and frozen vegetables have about the same amount of nutrients, with the exception of pumpkin and tomatoes, both of which are healthier canned rather than fresh. Canned foods sometimes get a bad rap, but they can be an easy side dish or addition to a soup or stew without the hassle of preparing their fresh counterparts. If you are concerned about sodium levels, pick frozen over canned.

Here are the canned staples for your pantry:

Artichokes—hearts, quartered: Use in main dishes, salads, and appetizers.

Cherries—pitted, whole: Use for pies, substitute for fresh.

Corn—sweet corn, creamed corn: Use as side dish, in salads and casseroles, can substitute for frozen.

Green beans—French cut, Italian cut: Not a substitute for fresh.

Green chili—mild, diced: Use in sauces, salsas, casseroles.

Hearts of palm—stalks, whole or sliced: Use in salads.

Mandarin oranges: Use for fruit salads, lettuce salads, and gelatin desserts.

Mushrooms—whole, sliced: Use for cooking, not a substitute for fresh.

Olives—whole, pitted, sliced: Use for cooking, salads, and appetizers.

Peaches/Pears—diced, whole: Use as a side dish or in pies.

Peas—field peas, black-eyed peas: Use in salads and side dishes, can substitute for fresh.

Pineapple—diced, rings: Use for snacks, side dishes.

Tomatoes—whole crushed tomatoes, tomato paste, diced tomatoes: Use in sauces, main dishes, can substitute for fresh for cooking.

CANNED FISH

Nutritionists tout the benefits of cold water fish as having high amounts of the essential fatty acid omega-3. If you like the taste of fish, adding it to your diet can be quite beneficial. Beware of the smell associated with an open can of fish and plan on plenty of complaints from the non-fish loving members of your household. Wrap the empty cans in a plastic bag and bury the bag in the garbage. Rinse the sink and all bowls immediately; that should help with the odors.

Anchovies: Salty, use on crackers, salad, and pizza toppings.

Salmon: Mix with mayonnaise for salmon salad.

Sardines: Small salty fish, substitute anchovy, herring, or mackerel (all found canned).

Tuna: Look for dolphin-safe tuna.

OLIVES

Cultivated for over 5000 years, olives are a pungent, salty food that evoke either wrinkled noses or big smiles. Olives are produced in many arid, sunny climates around the world. The olive is inedible unless it is cured, which occurs by soaking it in water, oil, brine, or lye. The final product should be meaty and soft. Dried olives have been cured in salt or olive oil. They will look shriveled and puny. Olives can be bought refrigerated or at room temperature in bottles or cans. Salty and sharp in flavor, olives are great served alone as an appetizer, tossed in salads, or added to a favorite recipe for extra flair. Having a variety on hand will give you many options (**8.3**).

Black olives: Small, medium, or large tree-ripened olives, usually pitted and canned.

Flavored olives: Olives cured in brine that has extra spices and herbs added. Use as appetizers, snacks, and for marinated salads.

Green olives: Unripened olives, usually pitted and stuffed with other ingredients. Use as appetizers and in salads.

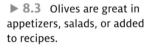

▶ **8.3** Olives are great in appetizers, salads, or added to recipes.

Kalamata olives: Large fully ripened Greek olives, pitted or unpitted. Pair them with feta cheese and tomatoes for a quick salad.

Martini olive: Pitted green olives stuffed with pimentos, use as snacks or drink garnishes.

Nicoise olives: Small fully ripened French olives. Usually bottled with pits, used in the famous Nicoise salad.

DRIED FRUITS

Dried fruits are loaded with antioxidants, vitamins, and fiber. Combine them with nuts for a great snack. Add them to breakfast cereals, muffins, and breads. Sprinkle in salads for a burst of sweetness. Purchase them in small quantities and store in resealable plastic containers. They can also be stored in the refrigerator, where they will become less sticky and stay plumper over time (**8.4**).

Dried apples: Use in breads, desserts, stuffings.

Dried apricots: Use as a snack and in baked goods.

Dried blueberries: Use in muffins.

Dried cranberries: Use in muffins, breads, cereals.

Dried dates: Use in desserts, stuffings.

Dried figs: Use in desserts, stuffings.

Dried mango: Use in snacks and desserts.

Dried pineapple: Use in muffins and breads.

Prunes (dried plums): Use in cooking and baking.

Raisins (dried grapes): Use as snacks, in cookies, muffins, and breads.

◄ **8.4** Refrigerating dried fruits will keep them moist.

VINEGARS

Vinegar plays a huge role in the world of cooking. It's added to salad dressings, marinades, sauces, and desserts. A couple of drops of vinegar can correct a sweet sauce. It's also the magic ingredient for pickling. Since vinegar is an acid, only use with stainless steel-lined pans and utensils.

Apple cider vinegar: A tangy, tart, fruity vinegar made from fermented apples. Mostly used in coleslaws, sweet and sour sauces, and marinades.

Balsamic vinegar: A fruity, sweet, mild vinegar that has been aged like wine. Quality and taste vary tremendously. Most supermarket varieties aren't true balsamic because they don't cost $100 a bottle. That said, they come close enough and are fine in most recipes. Look for white balsamic vs. red balsamic for a less acidic taste. Balsamics are great for salad dressings and marinades.

Champagne vinegar: Made from fermented champagne, its light taste is usually reserved for simple vinaigrettes.

Flavored vinegar: A wine or white vinegar that has been steeped with herbs, like tarragon, basil, garlic, or combined with peppers and/or spices. Intriguing flavors and colors make them fun to have and use for added taste to salads and sauces. They should be refrigerated after opening.

Fruit vinegars: A wine or white vinegar that has been steeped with fruit. The most popular flavor is raspberry. Fruit vinegar is usually added to sauces or dressings that warrant sweetness. Refrigerate after opening.

Malt vinegar: A very strong, sour vinegar made from malted barley. It's best known for sprinkling on fish and chips, a fried British dish. Good for pickling and making chutney, also Canadians are known to sprinkle it over French fries.

Red wine vinegar: A staple in French cooking, used in many vinaigrettes and sauces.

Rice wine vinegar: A sweet vinegar made from fermented rice. It's a staple in the Asian pantry. Its mild acidity makes it easy to add to many dishes when a bit of tang is wanted. Also try seasoned rice wine vinegar.

Sherry vinegar: A sweet, mild vinegar made from fermented sherry. It's similar in taste to balsamic and can be a good substitute.

White vinegar: A tart, clear vinegar mainly used for sauces, pickling, and salad dressings. Also used for cleaning products.

White wine vinegar: Not as popular as red wine vinegar and more subtle in its flavor. Used in cooked dishes.

STOCKS, BROTHS, AND BOUILLONS

It used to be you had two choices when it came to sauces or stocks: Make your own or use bouillon cubes. Now stocks are sold in cans and boxes. They are also sold as "glazes," which are available in a jar. Cooking with stocks can really add a gourmet taste to your dishes. Plan on paying a premium for these small containers, but rest assured, they are worth it. The time saved making them (a day in your life) and the small amount needed (usually a teaspoon) with each recipe should mitigate your concerns about cost. They have a long shelf life, up to a year. Once opened, the jars or boxes should be refrigerated. If you can't find them at your local gourmet store, there are many sources on the Internet to choose from.

Beef broth: Use as a base for gravies and sauces. Choose one that doesn't have too much sodium.

Bouillon cubes: Chicken, beef, vegetable, or ham—perfect in a pinch to add flavor to gravies or soups.

Bouillon in a jar: Better flavor and control when used to make stocks.

Chicken broth: Good to have on hand, but will need to be doctored up for a true chicken soup.

Concentrated beef stock: A glaze is a meat or fish stock that's been cooked for many hours until it's thick and rich with flavor. French cooks add dollops of it to their sauces at the last minute to thicken and boost their flavor. Also used to deglaze pans and form the basis of many gourmet sauces.

CONDIMENTS

Condiments can be any sauce or spread used to enhance a completely cooked dish. Since everyone has his or her favorite

Buying Bulk Foods

Many stores, like food cooperatives, offer bulk purchasing of grains, spices, dried fruits, chocolate, trail mix, nuts, and candy by the pound. The items are displayed in bins with plastic lids and scoops. This is a great way to get ingredients that you might not need in large amounts. Conversely, buying some staples, like rice or oats, by bulk can save you a lot of money. Price clubs also offer large-scale purchasing that has already been sealed and packaged. While shopping in these stores saves time (because each purchase will last longer) and often money, this only works if you have the storage space.

condiment, be sure your pantry stocks them at all times! Most jars have a long shelf life, so you can stock up when you find the items on sale. Don't forget: Always refrigerate after opening if the label says so.

Barbeque sauce: A tomato, vinegar, or mustard-based sauce that can be sweet, smoky, or spicy depending on what's added. Baste on cooked meats.

Chili sauce: A spicy tomato-based sauce with horseradish and other spices added, use in baked meat recipes.

Cocktail sauce: Tomato and horseradish sauce, use with shellfish.

Horseradish sauce: A creamy sauce with horseradish, use for meats.

Ketchup: A tomato-based sauce with vinegar, sugar, and salt. Use as a dip and an ingredient for other sauces.

Mayonnaise: A spread made from oil, egg yolks, and vinegar. Add garlic and call it aioli.

Mustard: Made from seeds ground and mixed with vinegar and spices. Varieties include yellow, Dijon, spicy brown, honey mustard, and gourmet varieties. Spread on sandwiches, use to make vinaigrette, or mix into a dipping sauce for chicken fingers.

Steak sauce: A caramel colored, thicker, tangy sauce. Used to flavor steaks.

Worcestershire sauce: A thin marinade developed in Britain, universally loved for its tangy sweet and sour flavor. The traditional contains anchovies and there are vegetarian options produced as well.

ASIAN PANTRY ITEMS

Asian ingredients are creeping into many recipes. In fact, soy sauce is considered a universal condiment as far as many cooks are concerned. Whether dry curry powder or coconut milk, they will add spice and flavor in different ways, so having some on hand gives you a leg up on creativity.

Black bean sauce: A staple of Chinese cooking, can be added to stir-fry.

Chili bean sauce: Fermented soybeans and chilies make a chunky condiment.

Chili paste: Various recipes blend a combination of hot chili peppers, garlic, salt, and oil.

Chili sauce: Used to flavor everything from soups to stir-fry.

Chutneys: Apricot, mango, or peach can be a sweet contrast to a spicy meat or curry dish. Use as a spread on breads as well.

Coconut milk: Juice made from strained coconut and added water, a main ingredient for curries.

Curry paste: Various combinations with chilies, garlic, and oil. Use as a base for making curry. Common curries are red, yellow, green, masaman.

Duck sauce: A sweet sauce used as a condiment to balance spicy dishes.

Fish sauce: A salty, pungent sauce used for soups and stews.

Garlic sauce: Similar to chili sauce, used to flavor everything from soups to stir-fry.

Hoisin sauce: A tart/sweet sauce used in stir-fry.

Peanut sauce: A spicy peanut-based sauce used as a dip or dressing.

Plum sauce: Thin, smooth chutney made from plums, use as a dip.

Soy sauce: Regular, low-sodium, wheat-free are common types. Use as a salty accent for cooking. Can also be used as a meat marinade because it will break down fat and make meat more tender.

PICKLES

Any vegetable can be pickled! But pickle eaters are picky! The flavors vary tremendously due to what is added to the pickling process. Some unopened pickles must be stored in the refrigerator. All of them must be refrigerated after opening.

Capers: Tiny flower buds, dried and pickled, they impart a flavor similar to green olive, with a touch of lemon. Use in salads and sauces and on top of bagels and smoked fish.

Cornichon: Tiny sweet pickle, the French version of a gherkin.

Gherkin: Small and pickled with sugar. Use in sandwiches.

Relish—sweet or dill: Diced pickles that can top hamburgers, hot dogs, or other meat sandwiches.

Sauerkraut: Canned or bottled pickled cabbage. A side dish or a topping for hot dogs and mustard.

OLÉ: MEXICAN SALSAS AND PEPPERS

The salsa market has exploded and there are plenty of brands to choose from. Look for salsas that have no added artificial ingredients. Store them in the refrigerator after opening. Canned peppers and tomatoes form the basis of many recipes, so stock up on your favorites.

Chipotle peppers: Use to flavor molés, sauces, dips, and salsa. Only one pepper is usually required. Leftovers can be frozen individually on a cookie sheet.

Corn salsa: A variation of tomatoes and corn or other vegetables, use as a dip or condiment.

Fruit salsa: Fruit added to tomatoes, use as a condiment for grilled or sautéed meats and poultry.

Mild pepper rings: Pickled peppers, use to spice up sandwiches, dips, and appetizers.

Pickled jalapeño peppers: Canned or in a jar, use in recipes requiring a bit of zing (**8.5**)!

Spicy pepper rings: Made similarly to mild pepper rings, only much hotter. Use on sandwiches.

Tomatillo salsa: Substitute for tomato-based salsa. Use in soups, enchilada dishes, and as a condiment.

Tomato salsa: Mild, medium, and spicy for different taste buds.

NUTS

Nuts are nature's perfect food. Got kids snacking on junk food? Try leaving a tin of salted cashews on the table and watch them disappear. Not only are they a high-protein snack loaded with vitamins and minerals, but they supply growing kids the good fats needed for brain development (**8.6**).

◀ 8.5 Pickled jalapeños, available in cans or jars, will certainly spice up a dish.

Since nuts contain a fair amount of oil, they should be stored in the refrigerator if they will not be eaten quickly. For long-term storage, place in freezer zip bags, label with the type and date purchased, and pile them in the freezer. They should last about six months. Nuts can be purchased shelled, unshelled, boiled, blanched, smoked, salted, and unsalted. If you are going to cook with them, make sure you get the type the recipe calls for.

Almonds: The most popular nut in the world, almonds are delicious salted, unsalted, smoked, blanched, and slivered. Use in salads and side dishes for a crunchy topping.

◀ 8.6 Nature's perfect food, nuts are tasty and healthy.

Cashews: A hardy crop grown in drier conditions, cashews have a dense, buttery texture. Use in stir-frys, such as chicken with cashews, or sprinkle over curry as a condiment.

Chestnuts: A meaty, mild nut harvested in the fall, the fresh chestnut is incorporated into many autumn and winter recipes, such as stuffings and stews. Fresh chestnuts must be roasted or boiled whole, then peeled.

Hazelnuts: A sweet, mellow-flavored nut used extensively in desserts with chocolate, they can be found whole, ground, or flaked.

Macadamia nuts: A creamy, crunchy nut grown mostly in Hawaii, they are expensive because they are difficult to shell. Used extensively in South Pacific cuisine, paired with pineapple and pork dishes.

Peanuts: Technically not a nut, but typically treated as such. Peanuts are inexpensive and high in protein. Used for making peanut butter and eaten as snacks, peanuts can add crunch to salads and sautés. Be aware that certain people have allergies to peanuts that can be fatal.

Pecans: A mild, sweeter version of a walnut, use in ice cream, pies, and desserts, try some candied pecans sprinkled in salads.

Pine nuts: Actually the seeds of a pine tree, pine nuts are highly perishable and hard to harvest, thus they are very expensive. They are a well-known ingredient for pesto. Sprinkle lightly toasted whole pine nuts over cream cheese for a quick snack.

Pistachios: Native to Asia, the nuts are small, extra crunchy, and delicious. They're sold shelled or unshelled and are quite expensive. Use in ice cream, cookies, soups and stews, or serve alongside curries and stir-frys.

Walnuts: Healthiest nuts on the planet, sprinkle them over cereals, bake them in bread.

HERBS AND SPICES

A large variety of dried herbs and spices is a must-have in any kitchen pantry. But you can't just get 'em and forget 'em. Spices begin to lose their flavor once they are ground. In supermarkets, they are often sold ground and there is no way to know how fresh they are. It's better to purchase small amounts of dried herbs and replenish as needed.

Herbs are the leafy part of the plant. Spices come from the bark, seeds, root, or fruit of a plant and can last a long time in your pantry, up to a year, before they're ground. Like coffee, they are easy to grind. Designate a small grinder just for your spices or grind them by hand with a mortar and pestle right before using. The aroma of fresh ground spices will convince you it's worth the effort.

Allspice: Also known as Jamaican pepper or pimento, it has a flavor reminiscent of cloves combined with nutmeg or cinnamon. Use in seasoning soups, stews, and curries. It is also used as a pickling spice, in desserts, and ketchups.

Anise: A grayish brown seed related to parsley, it has a licorice flavor. Use in soups, stews, and desserts.

Basil: Use the leaves, fresh or dried, in tomato sauces, and on grilled meats and vegetables.

Bay leaves: Harvested from a laurel tree and used as a dried whole leaf, they impart a subtle flavoring to soups, stews, and sauces. Remember to remove them from your dish before serving.

Caraway: Best known as the spice in rye bread, caraway seeds are also used in the stews and soups of Eastern Europe.

Cardamom: Tiny black seeds with a gingery, peppery flavor, they are pounded into a powder and added to Indian curries, soups, and stews.

Cayenne pepper: Hot and spicy. Use sparingly, usually after preparation is completed.

Celery: Light brown seeds from the celery plant, a member of the parsley family, used mostly in pickling recipes. Add it to salad dressings and soups for a bit of celery flavor.

Cinnamon: A dried bud used ground or whole in desserts, soups, stews. Very pungent, a little goes a long way.

Coriander: The tiny seed of the cilantro plant, used dried and ground in curries, soups, and stews, as well as in pickling and sausage making.

Cumin: An ancient spice from Egypt and the Mediterranean, the small green seed is usually ground. Cumin is a common ingredient in curry powders.

Dill: The leaves and seeds are used in chicken salad, cream sauces, cheese dips, and spreads.

Fennel: With a slight licorice flavor, fennel leaves and seeds impart less flavor than anise seeds. Use in fish dishes, sausage preparations, pickles, potatoes, and sauerkraut.

Fenugreek: Tasting like sweet celery, both the leaves and seeds are used in chutneys, meats, and vegetable dishes.

Galanga: Known as Thai ginger, it's a cousin of ginger used almost exclusively in Asian soups, curries, and stir-frys. Use dried, fresh, or ground.

Garlic: A member of the onion family, garlic can be used ground, or whole cloves can be minced, pressed, chopped, or mashed.

Ginger: A spicy, citrus peppered root that is peeled and then used dried or fresh.

Mace: A more pungent version of nutmeg, it actually is the ground outer covering discarded from the nutmeg itself. Use with sweet potatoes for a nutmeg flavor.

Marjoram: Tastes like mild oregano. Use fresh or use dried sprigs in stews, sauces, marinades, vinegars, oils, side dishes, and roast meats.

Mint: Mint leaves impart menthol when crushed. Use fresh to mix with cucumber, add to iced tea or lemonade, use dried for creamy soups, jellies, and sauces for roasted meats.

Mustard: Use white or yellow mustard seeds for pickling; yellow or brown for making homemade mustard.

Nutmeg: A subtle, fragrant seed that can be ground for use in pudding, pies, soups, and stews.

Oregano: The basis of Greek and Italian cooking. Use dry or fresh leaves to flavor tomato sauces, gravies, soups, and stews.

Paprika: A ground powder made from dried red peppers. Add to soups, stews, and casseroles, chorizo sausages, sprinkle on grilled meats, potato salad, and garlic bread. Paprika comes in a wide variety of flavors, including very spicy. The milder versions are used to add color to foods.

Parsley: A leafy green herb with a sharp taste, use dried or fresh leaves in salad dressings, marinades, add to mustard sauces, or sprinkle over cream sauces to finish a dish. Chew after eating to clean your breath!

Poppy: Tiny blue-gray seeds that impart a nutty flavor. Use to flavor breads, muffins, soups, stews, and sausages

Rosemary: Soft needle-like leaves that have a pine smell and flavor. Must be crushed or cut to release the flavors. Use fresh sprigs in sauces or dried leaves in soups, stews, and rubs for meat. Large branches can substitute for aromatic kabob sticks on the grill.

Saffron: The world's most expensive spice, it imparts a zesty, bitter flavor and adds yellow coloring to rice and other one-pot meals.

Sage: A cousin of mint, use ground in many marinades and seafood dishes. Add a tiny bit of fresh chopped leaves to dips and salads for a lot of tang.

Sesame: Sprinkle over stir-frys and vegetables for a subtle crunch. Toast on low heat to create a stronger flavor.

Tarragon: Its anise-like taste can quickly overwhelm a dish. Use the leaves sparingly to flavor vinegars, butters, and classic sauces like béarnaise and mayonnaise.

Thyme: Can be used in just about any recipe if you want to add a delicious flavor.

Turmeric: A root from the ginger family, it is usually steamed, dried, and ground. Adds flavor to curries and stews.

SALTS

Keeping a variety of salts on hand will make you feel like a true gourmet. Recipes that call for salt are usually referring to table salt, unless otherwise noted. Keep salt in an airtight container because it absorbs moisture readily. Coarse salts, like kosher salt, can be easily ground in a mill, just like pepper.

Celtic salt: A light gray, coarse sea salt, usually sold at a premium.

Kosher salt: A very coarse grind of salt. It has less sodium than table salt, a less salty taste, and the large crystals don't permeate food like finer-grained salts. Chefs like to cook with Kosher salt because it is easy to see and measure due to the large crystals.

Rock salt: A very coarse grind, used for making ice cream.

Sea salt: A coarse grind distilled from the sea. It usually contains trace amounts of minerals, which add to its unusual flavor.

Table salt: A fine-grain salt mined from dried-up lakes. Adequate for most recipes, but remember, a little goes a long way!

PEPPERCORNS

Pepper's ubiquitous use makes it seem like a humdrum ingredient. But there's a reason that fine restaurants bring peppermills to the table. Fresh ground pepper will give your cooking a huge burst of flavor. Mini peppermills the size of a spice jar can store various types of peppercorns and are easy to use.

Black peppercorns: The almost ripened berry, picked and dried, most pungent.

Green peppercorns: The unripened berry, but usually brined not dried, less pungent.

Red peppercorns: The fully ripened berry, dried, usually found in a multi-colored mix.

White peppercorns: The fully ripened berry with its red skin removed and dried, not as pungent.

SEASONING MIXES

You can find delicious bottles of combined herbs and spices that give dishes an authentic taste. And let's face it, sometimes you don't have time to make your own curry powder from scratch. To recreate a particular taste of a regional cuisine, many cookbook authors recommend specific brand name seasoning products in their recipes. Try to buy the one recommended, but if you can't find it, another similar seasoning in the same category should suffice. Below are descriptions of some basic combinations. The best part about making your own is that you can add more of your favorite flavors and omit those you don't care for.

Cajun/Creole seasoning: A blend of herbs and spices indigenous to the state of Louisiana. Mix ¼ teaspoon each of salt, paprika, pepper, onion and garlic powder, dry mustard, red and black pepper, file powder, dried thyme, and basil leaves. Use for gumbo and jambalaya.

Chili powder: A well-known spice combination used to make assorted meat dishes. Try 1 teaspoon paprika, cayenne pepper, oregano, and 2 teaspoons garlic powder and ground cumin.

Curry powder: A spice blend that changes depending on the region or country of origin. Try a blend of 1½ teaspoon each of ground ginger, ground turmeric, ground cumin, ground paprika, ground coriander seeds. Add ground cardamom seeds and ground cayenne pepper to taste (they are very pungent and distinct in flavor). Other spices to add are fenugreek, ginger, allspice.

Herbes de Provence: A famous French combination using herbs common from the hillsides of southern France. Picked fresh and then tied together with a string, they are used to flavor sauces, gravies, soups, and stews. Bottled herbs are dried combinations of thyme, marjoram, basil, rosemary, summer savory, and lavender. Mixed in a bowl with a little olive oil, they can be rubbed on meats and potatoes. Try this combo: 1 tablespoon each of dried basil, thyme, marjoram, summer savory, and rosemary. Add lavender buds to taste.

Italian seasoning: A combination of dried herbs typically used in tomato-based pasta sauces. Try this combination: 1 teaspoons dried basil, oregano, and marjoram, and ½ teaspoon dried sage.

Pumpkin pie mix: A shortcut combination including common spices used to make pumpkin pie. Combine ¼ teaspoon of ground cinnamon and ginger and ⅛ teaspoon of ground allspice and nutmeg.

Steak house dry rub marinade: Usually a combination of sweet, salty, bold, and spicy hot flavors. Try combining a teaspoon of sea salt, paprika, sugar, dried onion, powdered garlic, and black pepper. Add dry rosemary and basil for an Italian touch. Add dry oregano and lemon peel for a Greek seasoning.

■Marinades

Marinades serve two purposes: to season and to tenderize meat. Wet marinades rely on an acid or enzymes, such as vinegar, milk, or papaya, to break down tough fibers. Dry marinades or rubs use oil as a vehicle to spread the spices and penetrate the muscles. Purchasing store-bought marinades can really be hit or miss. Bottled marinades don't have the fresh flavor that homemade ones impart, and some dry marinades are full of chemicals. Most marinades can be quickly and easily made at home if you have a well-stocked pantry, so this is your best option. If you must buy one, stick with marinades that are a combination of easy-to-recognize ingredients. No need for added chemicals here.

COOKING OILS

If you think you can get by with just a bottle of vegetable oil, think again. Oils are best used for specific purposes and form the basis of many types of cuisines. Olive oil is the number one oil to have on hand. Not only is it healthy but it's very versatile (**8.7**). Try to go to a gourmet store where they have oil tastings and compare the different flavors. Most oils can be stored in the pantry opened for three to six months; however, oils from nuts are best stored in the refrigerator.

▶ 8.7 Olive oil is the most versatile oil to keep on hand.

The smoking point is the temperature at which an oil begins to smoke. Smoky oil is not good: it will ruin your dinner. Oil blends usually have lower smoking points than single oils. Unrefined oils usually have lower smoking points than refined oils.

Ever wonder why a recipe calls for a specific oil to use? It's not because it was the only oil in the author's kitchen! All oils have different characteristics that make them better or worse to use for different cooking techniques. For use in high-heat cooking, purchase oils with a high smoking point. For baking, use oils that impart little or no flavor to the recipe. For salads, flavorful oils are better choices. Another good rule of thumb is to use olive oil for low- to medium-heat dishes and canola oil for higher temperature frying.

Unrefined oils are called cold-pressed oils. Extra virgin olive oil is an example of cold-pressed oil. Refined oils are made through a hot-extraction process. Hot extraction methods include expeller pressed and solvent extraction. Common expeller-pressed oils are peanut, safflower, and sunflower. Solvent-expressed oils use a combination of solvents, bleach, and high heat methods to extract the oil, which creates flavorless, odorless, colorless oil. These oils are better for frying, searing, and grilling because the extraction method actually makes the smoking point higher after processing.

Canola: A light healthy oil, excellent for baking and salad dressings, good for frying.

Chili oil: A vegetable oil infused with chili seasoning, used as a condiment in Asian cooking.

Coconut oil: Hard at room temperature, a great substitute for shortening in baking, and thought to have beneficial properties for dieters.

Corn oil: Light, colorless oil that imparts a clean taste in baking. A high smoking point makes it good for frying.

Extra virgin olive oil: The most expensive olive oil so take the time to find one with a flavor you like. Use for light frying or sautéing, dipping breads, or drizzling onto finished dishes.

Flaxseed oil: A golden colored oil that imparts a buttery flavor, known for its high amount of omega-3s, which are very healthy for you.

Grape seed oil: A clean, flavorless oil with a high smoking point, use for frying or when minimal extra flavor is desired.

Peanut oil: Refined peanut oil has a high smoking point, making it excellent for frying. It doesn't leave any residual flavors on fried foods.

Sesame seed oil: Comes from sesame seeds that have been roasted before being pressed. Delicious nutty oil used to flavor stir-frys and dressings. Often very spicy, a little goes a long way.

Soybean oil: Highly refined with a high smoking point, inexpensive, and adequate for all uses.

Vegetable oil: Highly refined with a high smoking point, usually a combination of corn, soy, and sunflower oils.

Vegetable shortening: Vilified of late for its trans-fatty acids, vegetable shortening still makes the best flaky pie crust. New trans-free versions are on the market, but their performance does not compare to the real thing.

Virgin olive oil: Generic, lightly flavored oil used as a base for salad dressings and low-heat sautéing.

Walnut oil: Offers a distinct walnut flavor that tastes good in salad dressings.

MILK

Canned milk was developed when the fresh milk supply was unreliable and possibly contaminated with bacteria. So why have it in the modern pantry? Through trial and error, it was discovered that the milk proteins in canned milk, already subjected to high heat, are less likely to curdle or separate when used in cooking. This makes it ideal for use in puddings, pies, and sauces. Check for expiration dates when purchasing. Don't buy any cans that are dented or bulging. If you remember to flip the can over in the pantry every month or so, you can retard the milk solids from separating. Once they separate, throw it out: the product is not usable.

New technologies, such as ESL (extended shelf life) packaging let you purchase regular milk and keep it on your shelf. If you are looking for an alternative to regular milk due to dietary reasons, soy and rice beverages can also be purchased in ESL cartons and stored in your pantry. There are many cookbooks and Web sites that explore using soy and rice drinks as substitutes for milk.

SUGARS AND SYRUPS

Sugars usually find themselves part of most baking recipes, and they are also used in making such things as jellies, chutneys, and barbecue sauces. Since sugar has a long shelf life—up to two years, it's fine to stock up. Boxed sugars should be transferred to airtight containers to retard moisture absorption. Syrups are forms of liquid sugar and have a variety of uses in cooking and baking.

Brown sugar: White sugar with molasses added to increase moisture retention while baking.

Confectioner's sugar: Powdered sugar used for frostings and desserts.

Corn syrup: A sugary syrup made from corn, used in frosting and candy-making.

Honey: Made by bees from a blend of plant pollens, it's high in nutrients and sweeter than sugar.

Light brown sugar: Brown sugar with less molasses.

Maple syrup: Always refrigerate after opening.

Pancake syrup: Usually artificially flavored to mimic maple syrup.

White sugar: A fine-grained sugar used for all purposes in cooking.

OTHER BAKING INGREDIENTS

You can't bake without at least some of these important ingredients.

Baking powder: Used as a leavening agent, lasts about three months after opening.

Baking soda: Also works as a leavening agent, used in cakes and cookie recipes, lasts three months after opening. Also stick an open box in your fridge to eliminate odors.

Biscuit or pancake mix: Lasts about six months after opening. Store in a zippered plastic bag.

Cornstarch: Works as a binder or thickener in sauces, gravies, and puddings. Lasts about six months.

Cooking Techniques Everyone Needs to Know

Now that you *have a fabulously designed, totally organized, ultimately outfitted, stocked-to-the-brim kitchen, it's time to cook something. Never fear. Because you have forged this new bond with your kitchen, it's going to be easier than ever to make delicious meals for yourself, your family, and friends. So, let's tackle some of the issues about how to be a successful cook.*

Cooking is different from other pursuits in that the decision to make a particular dish can be founded on a whim, such as "I'm in the mood for pudding." There are no rules to follow except what your desires dictate, what your pocket can afford, how much time you have to spare, and how will it be accomplished. Being a cook requires you to translate a recipe and transform it into an edible dish, preferably delicious. This chapter is about demystifying the ins and outs of cooking in an easy, fun way so you can enjoy your kitchen to its fullest.

Step One: Pick a Recipe

Cooking should be a joyful, fun endeavor, so turn on some great music before you do anything else. Once you feel comfortable, locate the recipe you are interested in making and sit down for a few minutes. Read the recipe all the way through three times. The most common cooking mistake is misreading a recipe's instructions. The recipe will be easier to understand each time you read it. It will also give you a heads-up on the preparation time. For example, if you find a line that reads "marinate for 24 hours," pick something else if you are planning to cook that night's dinner.

Step Two: Check Your Equipment

Make sure you have the tools to complete the recipe properly. If the recipe asks you to sauté something, then you are going to need a sauté pan. If you are supposed to whip something, make sure you have an electric mixer and that you can find the whisk attachments! If using the oven, double-check inside to make sure it's clean. You don't want old drips to cause any smoke while preheating it.

Step Three: Assemble the Ingredients

The next thing is to locate all the ingredients. Check the expiration dates on products you already have. If something has been opened, physically check the ingredients for freshness. This is particularly important regarding herbs and spices since they can lose the pungency required to season the

1. Dress the part. Put on your apron and secure a dishtowel to the ties that wrap around your waste. This is a professional chef's way of quickly wiping his or her hands while he or she works.

2. Keep a second dishrag handy and use it to quickly wipe the prep area when moving from one step to the next.

3. Take out all the necessary ingredients. Refrigerated ingredients like milk, cheese, meat, and eggs should be left out to reach room temperature so they aren't too cold when added to a recipe.

4. Pre-measure your dry ingredients like flours, sugars, and spices. Make sure you've used a dry measure, not the liquid one.

5. Chop all your ingredients before adding any into the recipe. The size of an ingredient will determine just how fast it cooks. For example, a diced onion will cook much faster than a sliced one.

6. Preheat appliances. It will cut down on overall dish preparation time.

7. Make sure your dishwasher is empty. You don't want to be searching for a tool and find it dirty.

8. Turn down the thermostat. There is nothing worse than sweating into your food.

9. Determine the number of diners and adjust the recipe accordingly. Double portions or cut them in half as necessary. Use a calculator to help with the math.

10. Make sure knives are sharpened. It will greatly reduce the number of accidents while slicing and dicing.

dish properly. Also, make sure you have enough of everything. Make a list of what you don't have. Write down anything you need to purchase on your next trip to the store.

Step Four: Prep the Dish

Most of the time spent cooking is actually not the cooking part (unless it's risotto, where you stir and stir and stir, but that's another book). It's really the step before cooking, called prepping, that takes time and patience.

Step Five: Cook It

Most recipes don't tell you how to do something, just to do it. Maybe you have a vague notion of what it means and have always wondered: Is there a really difference between mincing and chopping? What about boiling and blanching? Beating and whipping? It's time to stop fudging it and learn how to do things properly. What follows are concise explanations of basic techniques that will get you through most recipes. The more you practice them, the easier and faster cooking will seem.

Cooking with Liquids

Amazingly, it's actually possible to cook a whole meal with just a pot of hot water. When you vary the temperature, you get a variety of techniques, notably boiling, blanching, poaching, and steaming.

BOILING

This is cooking thoroughly in a pot of boiling liquid. Corned beef and cabbage is an excellent example. Make sure the water is completely boiling before adding any food. Using a lid will make things boil faster. Once the boiling point is reached, the temperature can be lowered and still maintain the boil. Crack the lid or take it off, depending on the recipe. Adding a dash of salt before the water boils will make it boil at a higher temperature and reduce the overall cooking time.

PARBOILING

This mean partially boiling a vegetable until it is almost cooked. Used for dishes that require the vegetable to be further cooked using another method. For example, some potato dishes ask for potatoes to be diced and boiled so that the sauté part can be performed quickly.

BLANCHING

Blanching refers to partially cooking food in boiling water. In many stir-fry recipes, the instructions typically want you to blanch vegetables to make them tender before sautéing or frying. It's also used before freezing vegetables with enzymes that may destroy the flavor while sitting in the freezer. Blanching brings vegetables to their brightest color, and lasts for no more than a few seconds. For easier retrieval, put everything in a wire basket and cook it for the appropriate amount of time. You can either blanch by boiling (submerging the wire basket) or steaming (suspending the wire basket). This will vary depending on the food. When done, quickly submerge in an ice water bath to stop the cooking process.

Follow these general guidelines, but look at color and feel for tenderness to ensure proper doneness. The longer time pertains to steaming.

Asparagus: 3–4 minutes
Broccoli: 3–5 minutes
Brussels sprouts: 3–5 minutes
Cabbage: 1–2 minutes
Carrots: 3–3½ minutes
Cauliflower: 3–3½ minutes
Corn on the cob: 3–8 minutes
Green beans: 2½–3 minutes
Greens (spinach, kale, mustard, collard):
    2–2½ minutes
Peas: 1½–3 minutes
Peppers: 2–3 minutes

Save Some Water

If you are going to boil pasta for dinner, use the same water to blanch fresh vegetables. After blanching, sauté them in olive oil for an easy side dish.

POACHING

Cooking a food submerged in a simmering liquid is called poaching. First, prepare the liquid. Fill a large stockpot with broth, then add complementary seasoning and herbs, and let them steep while you bring the liquid up to temperature. Once the broth is barely simmering, add your chicken or fish and cook until done. The only way to see if it's done is to take it out with a slotted spoon and check it.

SIMMERING

Simmering is used when cooking soups, sauces, or stews for longer time periods. The food needs to be at a hot enough temperature to cook, but if it were at a regular boil, the liquids would evaporate much too rapidly. To simmer, bring a pot of liquid to a boil, and then reduce heat to low, where the surface bubbles ever so gently. Don't forget to stir so food doesn't stick to the bottom.

STEAMING

This is a method of cooking over indirect heat using boiling water. Steaming food eliminates added fats, so it's a favorite of dieters. To steam something, put some water in a pot and bring it to a boil. Place your food on a rack that sits above the water. Cover the pot and let it cook. Most vegetables cook quickly, so check for doneness starting around four or five minutes.

STEWING

Stewing is exactly like braising only much more liquid is added so that the final product is a soup, usually called, you guessed it, stew!

Cooking on the Stovetop with Dry Heat

Dry heat produces different results than cooking with liquids. In many cases, the timing is important, as well as keeping a close eye on what you're cooking.

BROWNING/SEARING

This is an important step in the process of making the most of a meat dish. By searing the meat over high heat, the more complex flavor compounds are released into the pan. These compounds form the basis of gravies and sauces. Most novice cooks make the mistake of not heating their pan high enough, thus the oil isn't hot enough to brown the food properly. But you can't crank up your burner temperature to get it hotter quicker. It's better for the pan to be preheated on a medium temperature and allow the oil time to get heated slowly. To test the temperature of the pan, dribble a drop of water on the surface and it should sizzle.

SAUTÉING

Sautéing involves high heat and perfect timing, so you'd better make sure you are paying attention (i.e., do not answer the phone while sautéing). Until you get the technique down, try simple recipes that involve only two or three ingredients.

For perfect sautéing, you need to know how hot and fast your burners will heat. Preheat the pan without any oils in it. Choose an aluminum-clad pan, not non-stick. When you think it's too hot and start to get nervous then it's probably perfect. Again, drop water on the pan and it should shimmy on the surface.

Add the oils and turn up the heat a bit more. Wait until you barely see smoke and immediately add your ingredients. This is where your prepping pays off! You have absolutely no time to cut anything at this point, nor take your eyes off that pan for a second! Once you've added your ingredients, the temperature of the pan will automatically adjust downward. Depending on how brown you want the exterior of your food dictates how long you cook it. Turn the heat down a notch after initial browning is complete. Stir often until your food is cooked through. Just when you think you've finished cooking, there's still one more step: deglazing the pan.

DEGLAZING A PAN

After sautéing, you should have bits of browned meat and seasoning left in the pan. Whatever you do, don't throw them out! What's in your pan is called "fond" in highbrow culinary circles and it's the magic essence that forms the basis for a delicious sauce.

Before you start, remove the food from the pan and cover to keep warm. Remove all but a couple of teaspoons of the fat from the pan. While the pan is still hot, you can add fresh herbs, shallots, or other flavors, and stir on low heat for a minute. Pour in a small amount of liquid (wine, broth, lemon juice, water, etc.). Using a wooden spoon, scrape off the bits and pieces stuck to the pan, swirling them into the liquid as you go. You can also deglaze a roasting pan by placing it over the burners once you've taken your meal out of the oven. Either way, you now have the base for a sauce for your dish...read on!

THE "WOW" FACTOR: MAKING SAUCE OR GRAVY

After you deglaze the pan, you're probably looking at a brown sauce with charred crumbs. I know what you're thinking— this mess is my fabulous sauce? Where's the "wow"? Actually, it should be quite tasty and you could strain it and serve it now, but there's more to do to make it even better.

To make a sauce, raise the heat in the pan to high, add wine, stock, or whatever you are using to the pan, half a cup at a time, depending how much time you have (tip—use low-sodium broth when reducing so it won't get overly salty). Use caution when adding alcohol to the pan. Only add it when it's not on the burner unless you want singed eyebrows. Bring the liquid to a boil.

An alternative is to keep simmering. Add any juices released from the meat. As you simmer, the liquid will reduce into a velvety sauce that should cling to the back of a metal spoon. Upon completion, you can whisk in a teaspoon of butter and make it extra rich, but skip this step if you are watching calories. Straining the sauce is optional, but check your recipe. Add additional seasonings if desired.

If you want to make gravy, add some cornstarch paste (cornstarch and water). After boiling for a few minutes the consistency will thicken. Taste and correct the seasonings.

CARAMELIZING

Usually associated with onions, caramelizing is cooking over medium heat until the internal sugars dissolve and the food browns. It's important not to use a high temperature because foods with high sugar contents will burn easily.

FRYING

Frying is one of those techniques that looks easier than it actually is. Frying is all about heat! It needs to be generated evenly throughout the bottom of the pan to heat the oil properly. It is doable if you make sure that all the elements for success are in place:

1. Use the right pan. This is where a flat-bottomed, high-sided stainless steel pan with the aluminum/copper core is an ideal choice. Whatever you do, don't use a non-stick pan. It doesn't make as crispy a crust.
2. Monitor the temperature of the oil. Using a thermometer, monitor the oil at all times and adjust the heat as necessary. Most recipes tell you what the temperature should be, usually between 325 to 375 degrees. Oil that is too hot will brown the food fast but the insides won't get done. Food that is fried in oil that is too cold absorbs the oil and becomes mushy.

3. Use the right oil. The oil must have a high smoking point, such as refined peanut oil.

4. Don't skimp on the oil. Pour in enough oil to cover half the food. For example, when frying chicken breasts without the bone, you'd need half the thickness of the breast. If it has bones, then use two inches or more.

5. Fry each side only once. The recipe should specify how long to fry each side. If it doesn't, then choose a different recipe or research the information on the Internet. This is one of the most important parts!

6. Cook in batches. Never crowd the pan, thinking it will be quicker. The food needs adequate space to cook properly, not to mention, the more food added to the pan, the quicker the temperature will drop. Place each batch on a tray in a preheated 200-degree oven, and leave it there until you're ready to serve.

7. Serve immediately. The crust will remain crisp for about 15 minutes and then it's just never the same. To reheat leftover fried foods, use the oven or toaster oven and not the microwave.

BRINING

If you like salty food and have a tendency to overcook meat when frying, roasting, or grilling, then brining is for you. The best meats to brine are fresh whole chickens, turkeys, and large cuts of pork. Don't brine a self-basting bird! To brine a meat, you must soak it in a salt-and-sugar bath. A good rule of thumb is 1 cup of salt plus 1 cup of sugar dissolved in 2 quarts of water. You may need a small plastic trashcan to submerge larger birds. Soak ½ to 1 hour for every pound of meat. Rinse the meat thoroughly and air-dry uncovered in the refrigerator. This will ensure that the skin will be crispy when cooked.

Using Your Oven

When you use the oven, heat surrounds the food in order to cook it. To get the oven to the right temperature, you are required to preheat. Always set a timer to make sure your food cooks for the right amount of time, and use a meat thermometer for meat or poultry dishes to make sure that they are thoroughly cooked. Otherwise, you are possibly exposing yourself and your family to bacteria.

BROILING

The only difference between broiling and grilling is the location of the heat source. In broiling, the heat source comes from above. In grilling, the heat source comes from below. Yes, outdoor grilling tastes different than broiled food, but the premise is still the same. The high heat sears the food's exterior quickly. Thus, you must be very attentive when broiling (or grilling). When broiling, make sure to adjust your oven racks to position the top of your food directly near the heat source for best results.

ROASTING

The two popular methods of roasting are either dry roasting or moist roasting. Dry roasting is used for more tender cuts of meat. The first step is to season the meat in a skillet, then brown it on all sides. Place the roast in a pan large enough so it isn't touching the sides. Do not add liquid. Place in the oven and roast according to the recipe's timetable. The number of minutes will correspond to the number of pounds of meat, generally between 20-30 minutes a pound. This is when your meat thermometer comes in handy. The internal temperature of the roast will determine whether it is rare, medium, or well done.

When done, don't immediately cut into the meat. It will release the juices, which you want to keep inside.

Moist roasting uses moist heat to cook the meat. The meat is placed in the oven, and water, bouillon, or wine is added to the pan. You can make an aluminum foil tent over the roast, making sure it isn't touching the meat. Take two sheets of foil and fold one end over the other. Fold it again. This becomes a seal and doubles the width. The seam will be on top of the roast. Seal the fold all around the sides of the pan to keep the steam inside. It's easy to insert your thermometer into the seam. Make sure to angle the thermometer so you can read it. Cook according to the desired doneness. For both methods, let the meat rest for 15 minutes before carving.

COOKING TECHNIQUES EVERYONE NEEDS TO KNOW

Braising can be done on the stove or in the oven. It is an excellent way to cook tougher cuts of meat. While cooking, the collagen in the meat melts to yield a tender dish. To start, you will need a large covered skillet. Typically, you dredge the meat in a little flour, and then brown it on all sides. Pour off any extra fat and then add the braising liquid, usually a combination of any of the following: wine, broth, tomato sauce, or water. Add your seasonings and cover. Cook over low heat either on the stovetop or in the oven until the meat is tender. Watch your liquids and add more if they evaporate before the meat is cooked. When the meat is done, remove it and use the extra liquid to make a reduction sauce or gravy.

Microwaving

When microwave ovens were first introduced, they were supposed to be the answer for everything. My parents were the first people on the planet to buy a microwave oven. Thus my brother and I were guinea pigs for many disastrous experiments involving rubbery chicken, exploding oatmeal, burnt chocolate fudge, and a popcorn fire. My mom forged on with soggy green bean casseroles and tasteless meatloaf. It must have happened to many other families because the backlash was pretty severe. The word was out—microwave cooking had no taste!

These days, most people use their microwaves timidly, for heating up a cold cup of coffee. But in reality, if you use it properly, it is an indispensable tool—excellent for very specific uses. A word of caution is necessary in regards to boiling water in the microwave. Instead of boiling, the water particles are really jumping and bumping into each other. These move quickly and you can get burned. Instead, place a container three times the volume of the water to contain it. Also, a wooden spoon placed inside the cup helps keep it from boiling over.

You can use the microwave as the tool of choice for any of the following tasks:

Bake a potato.

Cook frozen vegetables.

Steam fresh vegetables.

Cook grains and rice.

Defrost meats, fish, poultry.

Heat tortillas.

Melt chocolate and butter.

Pop popcorn.

Reheat rice, or any takeout leftovers (as long as they are not in metal containers). However, avoid reheating pizza or anything fried—you're better off in the toaster oven.

Special Cooking Equipment

Some people like to cook with pressure cookers and slow-cookers. Both are worth mentioning because they offer the ease of one-dish cooking and virtually no cleanup except for the pot used.

PRESSURE COOKER

▲ 9.1 Use a pressure cooker to flash-cook your foods with steam.

A pressure cooker uses the pressure of steam to flash-cook foods that typically would take longer with traditional methods (**9.1**). It can easily pinch-hit for braising or stewing. The pressure increases the temperature, which cooks the food much faster. Because liquids and vapors aren't allowed to escape, flavors intensify, yielding delicious dishes. Some people are afraid of pressure cooking because there is a possibility of it exploding, but if you always release the pressure before unlocking the lid, you'll never have a problem Always check the seal of the lip before using the cooker and follow the manufacturer's instructions for maintenance and cleaning procedures.

SLOW COOKER

Slow cookers or crockpots cook by heating a lidded, glazed ceramic cooking vessel (**9.2**). Low or high heat is selected and the timer is set depending upon how long is needed. It's easy to throw together soups and chilies in the morning and have dinner ready that evening. The timer will turn the pot off automatically when the food is done. Be sure to follow the instructions carefully. Many Web sites are devoted to slow cookers and can yield more than a handful of inspirational recipes.

▲ **9.2** Slow cookers allow you to cook your meals throughout the day while you're working.

TOP BAKING TIPS

1. Always measure dry ingredients in a dry measure and make sure that you level off the top. Use the "scoop and sweep" method of measuring: Put the measuring cup into the dry ingredient and scoop it out, making sure it's overly full. Use a straight edge (knife, chopstick, or finger) and sweep it across the top, knocking off the excess so it's perfectly even with the top edge. If the recipe calls for it to be packed, gently press down with the back of a spoon as you fill the cup.

2. When you measure wet ingredients, use a heat-proof glass measuring cup. Keep the cup on the counter and eyeball the line, making sure it's exact, not over or under the line.

3. Milk, eggs, and butter should be at room temperature for most recipes. At room temperature, butter will give a little when pressed. Eggs can be warmed up in a bowl of warm water.

4. Prep the pan before you begin! Grease, flour, or line with parchment paper. All methods make releasing your creation easier.

5. Don't rely on the oven to have an accurate temperature. Use an instant-read thermometer and check for accuracy through the glass door because opening it will cause all the heat to escape.

6. Don't bake too much at once. Limit it to three cake pans and two large cookie sheets. Stagger them on different racks. To ensure even cooking, switch their positions and then turn them 180 degrees when they are halfway done.

7. Move the racks into place before you preheat the oven! No need to risk burns or heat your entire kitchen trying to adjust them once the oven is hot.

8. Non-stick baking pans or cookie sheets with dark surfaces yield better browning.

9. Don't substitute solid fats (butter or vegetable shortening) for a liquid fat (oil). Avoid using reduced-fat butters or margarines because they usually contain water. Don't grease the pan unless your recipe calls for it. Cooking sprays with flour are a great way to reduce calories.

10. Allow everything to cool thoroughly before storing. If it's covered while still hot, steam will form and ruin your efforts.

Baking 101

There's no reason why the average home cook can't make delicious cakes and cookies in the privacy of his or her own kitchen. Baking is easy to learn. Unlike cooking, baking is much more exact. Following the recipe will usually ensure success.

DIET-FRIENDLY BAKING

No need to cut out dessert; just cut out some calories in whatever you prepare! Most recipes can be modified to restrict calories and still turn out delicious. The trick is to maintain the original texture and sweetness of the dessert.

Cut the sugar: A cup of sugar is 360 calories. But, if you replace all the sugar with a sugar substitute, it won't brown correctly or have a good texture. Experiment with replacing ½ to a ⅓ of the sugar with a sugar substitute that is marked for baking, and see if you like the final results.

Cut the fat: Replace half the fat (shortening or oil) with the same volume of applesauce or pureed prunes. Replacing a whole egg with two egg whites will eliminate 5 grams of fat.

Add fiber: Substitute ½ the white flour with whole wheat flour.

Conversions and Measurements

Knowing about common measuring terms, abbreviations, measuring equivalents, and conversions is crucial. Here's what you need to know.

U.S. SYSTEM OF MEASURE

tsp or t = teaspoon
tbsp or T = tablespoon
c = cup
pt = pint
qt = quart
gal = gallon
oz = ounce
fl oz = fluid ounce
lb = pound
F = degrees Fahrenheit

METRIC SYSTEM OF MEASURE

g = gram
l = liter
ml = milliliter
m = meter
C = degrees Celsius

LIQUID MEASURING CONVERSIONS

1 gal = 4 qt = 8 pt = 16 cup = 128 fl oz = 3.79L
½ gal = 2 qt = 4 pt = 8 cup = 64 fl oz = 1.89L
¼ gal = 1 qt = 2 pt = 4 cup = 32 fl oz = .95L
½ qt = 1 pt = 2 cup = 16 fl oz = .47L
¼ qt = 1/2 pt = 1 cup = 8 fl oz = .24L

DEFINING "A PINCH"

No, a pinch isn't what you get on the cheek from a long-lost relative. It's a highly technical term involving precise measurement of a minute ingredient. Cooking is fraught with terms like "a pinch" and "scant" and nobody really ever explains them. So they need to be explained.

Pinch = ⅛ tsp or less
Scant = less than the exact equivalent (Confused? A scant teaspoon is "almost a teaspoon," just a bit less!)
Dash = two or three drops

Food Substitutions

When you're caught short, a substitution can save the day, or at least avoid a long interruption and a trip to the store. Here are some useful ones when you're down on ingredients:

1 tbsp Arrowroot = 2 tbsp flour or 1 tbsp cornstarch
1 oz chocolate = 3 tbsp cocoa powder + 1 tbsp melted butter
1 tbsp corn starch = 2 tbsp flour
1 medium egg = 2 egg yolks + 1 tbsp water (for recipes with flour only)
1 cup buttermilk = 1 cup milk + 1 tbsp lemon juice or white vinegar (let stand 5 minutes)

1 tbsp baking powder = ¼ tsp baking soda + ½ tsp cream of tartar

1 tbsp fresh herbs = ½ tsp dried herbs

1 cup milk = ½ cup evaporated milk + ½ cup water

1 cup light cream = ⅞ cup whole milk plus 3 tbsp butter

Cookbooks

I can usually peruse a new cookbook and decide quickly whether or not I want it. A seasoned cook who's logged years in the kitchen might look for a cookbook with challenging techniques and exotic fare. A beginning cook, however, might be looking for concise instructions and the ability to pronounce all the ingredients! With the thousands of cookbooks published each year, you need to be judicious in your choices.

What exactly makes a good cookbook? It should contain the following:

1. Recipes that spark your imagination and enthusiasm.
2. Interesting combinations of ingredients.
3. Easy-to-follow instructions, preferably contained on one page.
4. Recipes that are presented in an intelligent manner, not cute or fun.
5. Specialty ingredients that are discussed beyond just listing them.
6. Chapter headings that make sense—nothing fancy is best.
7. An accurate index with cross-referencing of main ingredients.
8. Suggestions for equipment needed, such as "Fill a 10-quart stock pot" instead of "Fill a pot."
9. As many pictures as possible—visuals show the author's true intentions.
10. Nutritional analysis with calorie breakdowns.

I've compiled a list of favorites. Some are old, some are new, and some are old and newly reissued.

COOKING 101

Basic recipes, techniques, a "how to" reference cookbook.
The Joy of Cooking by Irma S. Rombauer

New Cookbook by Better Homes and Gardens
The New Basics Cookbook by Julee Rosso and Sheila Lukins

GOURMET CLASSICS

Cookbooks with popular recipes that have been updated.
Silver Palate Cookbook and *Silver Palate Good Times
    Cookbook* by Julee Russo and Sheila Lukins
The Williams-Sonoma Kitchen Library series
The Martha Stewart Living Cookbook by Martha Stewart
    Living Magazine
The Way to Cook by Julia Child
The Barefoot Contessa Cookbook by Ina Garten
The Uncommon Gourmet by Ellen Helman
Perla Meyer's Art of Seasonal Cooking by Perla Meyers

TIME IS OF THE ESSENCE

Cookbooks that make delicious food simple or fast using
a short ingredient list, usually basics you should have in
your pantry.
30-Minute Meals by Rachel Ray
Six Ingredients or Less: Slow Cooker by Carlean Johnson
Keep It Simple: 30-Minute Meals From Scratch by Marian Burros

VEGETARIAN COOKING

Cookbooks that showcase vegetarian recipes.
Moosewood Cookbook by Mollie Katzen
Vegetarian Epicure by Anna Thomas
1,000 Vegetarian Recipes by Carol Gelles

ETHNIC CUISINE

Cookbooks that specialize in native or cultural dishes of a
specific country.
Essentials of Classic Italian Cooking by Marcella Hazan
*Glorious French Food: A Fresh Approach to the French
    Classics* by James Peterson
Sky Juice and Flying Fish: Traditional Caribbean Cooking by
    Jessica B. Harris
Keo's Thai Cuisine by Keo Sananikone
Mexico the Beautiful Cookbook by Susanna Palazuelos

REGIONAL CUISINE

American cooking from different parts of the country.

Frank Stitt's Southern Table by Frank Stitt, Pat Conroy, and Christopher Hirscheimer

Nantucket Open-House Cookbook by Sarah Leah Chase

Chef Paul Prudhomme's Louisiana Kitchen by Paul Prudhomme

Colorado Cache Cookbook by the Junior League of Denver

True Grits by the Junior League of Atlanta

BAKING

Helpful because desserts can be such an exact science.

The Cake Bible by Rose Levy Beranbaum

International Chocolate Cookbook by Nancy Baggett and Martin Jacobs

The Cake Mix Doctor by Anne Byrn

HEALTHY HOME COOKING

Always good for yourself and your family.

A New Way to Cook by Sally Schneider and Maria Robledo

Cooking Light Annual Recipes Cookbook by Cooking Light Magazine

ENTERTAINING

A quick way to become the perfect hostess or host.

Southern Living Easy Entertaining by Southern Living Magazine

Thanksgiving 101 by Rick Rodgers

COLLECTOR'S ITEMS

Expensive, beautiful cookbooks for the coffee table and serious cooks. You may have to hunt for these.

Larousse Gastronomique French by Prosper Montagne

Pacific Northwest the Beautiful Cookbook and others in the series by Kathy Casey, et. al

The French Laundry Cookbook by Thomas Keller

10

Entertaining with Ease

There are two types *of people in the world: those who entertain and those who don't. The "don'ts" will give every excuse in the book why they can't throw the party at their home, including "it's too small," "it's not decorated," or "we don't have enough serving stuff." What they are really saying is either a) they hate to throw parties, or b) they won't do it until they feel that everything is perfect. Well, guess what? If you worry about perfection, you'll never do anything.*

Life is so full of distractions and commitments that making your home perfect gets routinely pushed down the priority totem pole. And it should.

A great party doesn't happen in a perfect home. But having a great kitchen sure does help. So now that you have one, put it to use and throw a party! Whether it's for six or sixty people, entertaining with ease is within your grasp. However, there are several steps you need to take to ensure that the event runs smoothly.

Create a Theme

You don't need to have a reason for a party, but the best parties usually serve some purpose. Parties are often thrown for special occasions, like engagements or birthdays. These events mark important days in people's lives, and celebrating them can enhance their memories forever.

If you aren't celebrating a milestone, think of another reason to get your friends or family together. Remember, a theme doesn't mean a costume party. Most people want to be comfortable when they are socializing. After a cold February, my neighbor and I wanted to throw a party heralding the coming of spring. The invitations read, "Come to a chili supper to end the chilly season!" It was just the touch needed to make a casual get-together a special occasion to celebrate. Whatever your reason, you can incorporate different aspects of your theme right into the party planning.

Keep It Simple

Now that a theme has been established, stop. You heard me. Let the idea sit for a day and see if you still want to pursue it. It's easy to go overboard. An active imagination can produce grandiose plans, envisioning a formal soirée for 200 of your closest friends. But just thinking about a party on that kind of scale can easily overwhelm anyone, sending you diving under the covers of your bed, waxing on about everything that could go wrong. Then you end up doing nothing.

The real key to throwing a great party is entertaining while you are having fun yourself during every stage. That means you have to have fun planning a party so your guests will eventually enjoy the outcome. If you are worrying about everything, you'll be miserable. And the guests will sense it!

To keep it simple, scale down the guest list. By inviting fewer people, you can pare down the menu to include dishes that are easy to shop for and prepare. Also keep in mind how much time you are willing to devote to planning. Set up a time and money budget for your party and be honest about what you are realistically going to spend on both.

Enlist a Friend

If you have never thrown a party, get help. There is always a friend who will enthusiastically pitch in. From cooking to shopping, it will go a lot faster. When planning our chili supper, my neighbor and I split the tasks in half. She cooked two types of chili. I picked up the bread, wine, and paper goods. She made the brownies for dessert and I made the salad. The day of, our husbands pitched in with setting up chairs and tables on the patio. The kids filled coolers full of drinks and it was done.

The Invitation: Call or Write?

A written invitation is really the way to go. First of all, most people are pretty busy and a phone call to someone when they are distracted might not register. It's a lot to ask someone to get up during their favorite TV drama, go to their calendar, and actually write something down! And it's always fun to get mail, especially when you are opening an invitation. It makes the event stand out and marks the date in your guests' minds. If you must phone, it's actually better to call when you can leave a message on their answering machine. That way all the information can be replayed and double-checked for accuracy.

An invitation needs to contain the day, date, time, and place. Also, note who is throwing the party and who to RSVP to. The RSVP is crucial because the number of people attending will influence the amount of food, place settings, and seating that will be needed. Set a cut-off date for the RSVP, at least five days before the party. That's when you'll start your final planning.

Pick out a card or paper that echoes the theme you've chosen. There are many stationery shops that carry printed, "fill-in-the-blanks" invitations and specialty computer papers that allow you to create your own invitations. If you are computer savvy, come up with your own wording and print it at home. Purchase more invitations than you need in case the printer jams and ruins some of them. Make sure not to transpose any numbers while writing out the invitation. Check spelling and layout using the Print Preview function of your word processor. Print some first on blank paper and see if you need to make any changes.

Think outside the box: Why not take a few minutes and write a poem or joke pertaining to the theme? The invitation surely will be remembered. Here is an invitation I wrote for my father-in-law's 70th birthday party:

> There is a time for song and dance
> When birthdays strike a man
> To set a date and make a plan
> To gather all the clan
> So friends and family, please join us
> At a party for Daddy Dear
> It's Fred's birthday bash,
> He'll be seventy this year!
> The catch is that you mustn't say
> A word of this about
> It's a big surprise and he'll be floored
> If you contain your shout
> Now you know the big ta-do
> Is to celebrate in style
> Please RSVP to us real soon
> And we'll add your name to the pile.

> When: April 17
> Time: 6:00 PM
> Where: Naked Fish
> What: 70th birthday

> *Shhhhh! It's a surprise.*

Basic Invitation:

What: _____

Where: _____

Date: _____

Time: _____

Given by: _____

Please RSVP by (date): _____

Telephone: _____

Directions: _____

Cooking Considerations

This is the fun part, but again don't get carried away. Here's where you must mutter "keep it simple" one hundred times. If you are planning a cocktail party with party platters, limit the types of food to those that only need fingers or forks. Forget trying to cut meat on your lap! And where do you put the knife: dangling on the edge of a chair, about to fall on the floor? If you plan to serve salads, they need to be well-shredded and pre-dressed. Choose a variety of rolls instead of breads that need to be sliced. Desserts can be small pastries or chocolate-dipped fruits, etc. Avoid large messy cakes: they are hard to control when transferring to a small plate.

If your party has a theme, the food should echo it. A Cinco-de-Mayo party might include a choice of daiquiris, Mexican appetizers, and a build-your-own-taco bar. Check out the Internet or cookbooks for theme-based menus.

When setting the menu, you also need to consider the number of people attending and the time involved in preparation. Most entertaining gurus will tell you that if you like to try new recipes, now is *not* the time! But if you've never entertained, you're not going to have a huge cache of favorite standbys to pull your menu from. What to do?

First, any new recipe should be made at least once before it's served publicly. There are too many variables in cooking to leave it to chance. Better to try it on immediate family members instead. They can surely give you an honest opinion about how good it is.

Second, go with what you like. Pick recipes that reflect your very own tastes. Last year, I decided to make a healthy appetizer for a dinner party. I picked a low-fat artichoke dip. When I read the ingredients, it seemed like it might be bland, but I gave it shot. Well, it was bland! I then tried to doctor it up with extra flavor, but nothing worked. I felt like dumping it in the garbage, but I didn't have a substitute. Instead, I bit my tongue and had to serve it anyway, even though I didn't really like how it came out. Next time, I'll serve something that tastes good to me, and hopefully my friends will like it as well.

Pick recipes that have a short list of ingredients. One of my favorite cookbooks has recipes with only five ingredients each. A quick glance through the list will tell me if the combination of ingredients sounds good to my palate. And with such a short list of ingredients, prep time is inevitably reduced.

■Setting the Menu

Appetizers are a natural choice for larger-scaled parties. Make sure to pick ones that are easy to prepare and serve. There are plenty of delicious appetizers beyond the standard chips and dips. Avoid recipes that require food to be piping hot, unless you want to hide in the kitchen the entire time, sweating in front of the oven. Make some food a few days ahead and serve it in a user-friendly style. Don't force your guests to arm wrestle getting to the hors d'oeuvres. Set up platters in a few separate areas around the room. Each table should have its own pile of plates and napkins, so guests won't have to go on a search mission to find them.

Buffets

A buffet is a practical and flexible way to serve food to a large crowd. For starters, guests will feel more in control if they are not limited to a formal seating arrangement, and they can eat and socialize at their own pace.

The kitchen is a great place to stage a buffet. Set the food up using the island, a long stretch of counter space, the kitchen table, or a combination of any of these. Place the plates at the beginning of the table and the silverware at the end. Be sure to offer large plates: it's no fun looking at a spread of food and holding a tiny plate, knowing that you'll have to layer the food just to get it to fit. Use oversized napkins: when unfolded, an oversized napkin is big enough to spread across your lap while eating. It's elegant and efficient.

Staging a Buffet

Leave the drinks and cups off the buffet table: it's better to serve drinks from another area and stage dessert at yet another table. This creates the most important element of a good party—the flow. Making people move away from the food to get to another part of the meal encourages conversation.

BUFFET CHECKLIST

Make sure you have each of these items before setting up your buffet party:

Baskets, lined with cloth, for breads and crackers
Butter dish
Cake server
Cake stand with cover
Cheese board
Cheese knives, one for each type of cheese
Forks, twice as many as the number of guests
Gravy boat and spoon for sauces
Large serving bowls
Napkins
Plates, large and small, twice as many as the
   number of guests
Salad tongs
Serving platters for appetizers and meat dishes
Small decorative plates for olives, fruits, and vegetables
Smaller bowls for salsas and dips
Trivets for hot plates

The Sit-Down Dinner Party

If you are going to throw a more formal dinner party, choose the number of guests based on how many people your tables can comfortably accommodate. If you have a small dining table, consider renting a larger table instead of cramming everyone in.

If this is your first dinner party, I suggest that you serve it buffet style, but with seat assignments. A formal dinner requires the added pressure of trying to get everyone their food while it is still hot. A buffet eliminates being a waitress and you can concentrate on being a hostess, a job you're new to, and one that requires enough work as it is! You can still set the table as you would for a formal meal. Name cards mark where the hostess wants guests to sit. A wise hostess makes sure all the talkers don't sit at one end of the table!

The menu may vary but stick to a salad or appetizer that can be plated and on the table as guests sit down. That way you don't have to immediately disappear into the kitchen. Have a guest help pour the wine, and sit and enjoy! When the salad is finished, clear the plates and invite your guests to serve themselves from the buffet. Later, dessert can be served at the table by removing the centerpiece. Guests can continue to relax while coffee is brewing, and they can help themselves to dessert.

Setting the Table

Don't try to cram too many place settings on a table. People need room to eat! Consider extending the eating area by using a folding table and covering it with a matching tablecloth. For a formal table, you'll need the following (**10.1**):

Table linens: Tablecloths should be natural materials, not plastic! Cloth napkins can match exactly or contrast. Start with a basic white tablecloth. On top, diagonally layer another tablecloth in a different color, one that reflects the theme of the party (yellow for a baby shower, etc.). Another option is to use placemats. These can also be layered over a white tablecloth for an elegant, tailored look.

Napkin rings: Napkin rings hold the cloth napkins and allow them to be decoratively placed on top of or next to the plates. If you don't have many of your own, use a little imagination and create some (see chapter 5, for instance). For a graduation party, a simple tassel wrapped around the napkin would be fun and appropriate. For a birthday party, a single curling ribbon tied in a bow can make a decorative napkin ring.

◄ 10.1 A charger, a white plate, and a napkin ring contribute to a glamorous place setting.

Charger: A charger is an oversized decorative plate that sits under the dinner plate. Available in many colors and materials, it really adds to a glamorous place setting. It usually stays in place until the entrée is finished.

Dinner plate: Invest in a stack of white dinner plates. Food really looks fantastic on white, which is why it is a staple in many fine restaurants. It will also complement what you already own, in case you need to mix and match for a larger party.

Salad plate: Use a smaller plate that holds either a salad or the first course. Here's a chance to get creative. An interesting salad plate lends some contrast to the white dinner plate.

WINE GLASSES

Knowing about stemware is important because, surprisingly, certain wines taste better in certain glasses. Here's a quick tour:

Champagne: A champagne glass is referred to as a flute. It is tall and thin to keep the bubbles from escaping, ensuring that the champagne won't go flat.

Red wine: A large wide-rimmed globe that holds at least 6 oz of wine when only half full. Red wine needs to be exposed to oxygen to properly develop. As it airs, the range of flavors emerge.

White wine: Typically a medium-sized oval-shaped globe with a stem, these are smaller than red wine glasses and have a smaller mouth opening as well. Fill white wine glasses two-thirds full.

Water goblets: Large glasses that hold at least 6–8 oz of water (so not precisely a wine glass). A water goblet has a stem, like a wine glass, and looks more formal than your everyday barware.

FLATWARE

Only put out what you are going to use. If you aren't serving soup, don't put out a soup spoon. The rule of thumb is a guest should use the utensils from the outside and work his or her way towards the plate for each course served. For example, the salad or appetizer fork is placed on the left of the main course fork.

Forks: Put out small forks for salads and appetizers, large forks for the main course. For luncheons that have only one course, use the larger forks, even if you are only serving salad. They tend to be more comfortable for most people to maneuver.

Knives: If serving meat that has been carved, substitute a dinner knife for a serrated steak knife. Or bring additional knives out when the main course is served if a dinner knife was required for the salad or appetizer.

Spoons: Soup spoons are placed outside of the dinner knife, followed by teaspoons. Dessert spoons are placed centered above the plate.

■The Centerpiece

A centerpiece can be anything at all. It can reflect the seasons, be part of the party theme, or just be some funky, cool thing you put together. To create your own arrangement, start with the right container. Use a decorative planter, a crystal bowl, something that will stand out. Fill it with one large item and a smaller one for contrast and interest. A tower of lemons submerged in water held in an interesting glass vase makes a beautiful statement. A long ceramic tray can float candles and have colored marbles or polished stones at the bottom.

Just make sure the scale is in proportion to the table. If it's too big, you won't see your guests. If it's too small, it will look dinky. Experiment adding and subtracting things until you get a sense of what looks best. Add some low candles around the centerpiece to enhance the decorations.

Creating Atmosphere:
Music, Lighting, Decorations

The mood of the party should reflect the occasion. Don't overlook how atmosphere can really set the mood. There's a reason that balloons and streamers are practically universal at parties. They add excitement! With color, lighting, and music, you can put your guests in the right mood as soon as they enter the room.

LIGHTING

Lighting can single-handedly change the mood from everyday to special-occasion (**10.2**). People look better in dimmer lighting. If you have dimmer switches, use them! If you don't, turn off all overhead lights and use only lamps or lots of candles. Harsh bathroom lights should be turned off. Instead, leave a candle burning in the bathroom. Always place candles in a container or candle holder, and skip them entirely if small children are attending the party.

DECORATIONS

Decorations need to be considered during the early planning stages. Order flowers ahead of time and make small arrangements to scatter around the house. Anything can pinch-hit as a vase. Stick with single color blooms, like white or

◄ **10.2** Candles and an appropriate centerpiece can set the mood you'd like.

peach, for an elegant feel. Multi-color stems with lots of greenery give off a party atmosphere.

Don't underestimate how ribbons, crystals, and fabrics can set off an arrangement. Visit a fabric store and head straight to the discount table. Get some fabric in the colors you want and use it for table or chair swags and wall streamers. White fabric would work great for a white tie party, a wedding shower, or even a toga party!

MUSIC

Pre-select your music and load your CD changer before the party starts. Music transmitted through the television or computers can be coordinated into various rooms. Whatever vehicle you select, make sure that the same music is playing throughout your space.

For formal parties, lower the volume and play jazz or classical music. Stick with instrumental recordings so that lyrics won't compete with conversation. For birthday parties, select music from the guest of honor's favorite era or one that reflects his or her age. It's always fun to hear music from your past. For holiday parties, don't just grab the first holiday CD you can find. There are some really unique instrumental or ethnic sounding versions of typical holiday songs that would be equally, if not more, interesting.

Preparing for the Party

THE WEEK BEFORE

Get your lists together: Put together your recipes from the party menu. Double-check the pantry and refrigerator for all the supplies, making sure they are fresh and not past expiration. Create shopping lists for food, beverages, decorations, and ice! If you are missing crucial things, like a wine opener, put it on a list.

Inventory the serving dishes: Designate a serving dish for each menu item. Note the quantity that will be needed and make sure the vessel will hold whatever you'll be making. Think outside the box for inventive ways of displaying food. One of my friends filled a plastic baby tub with ice to hold cold drinks for my baby shower.

Plan the traffic flow: If you are always tripping over that small sculpture in the foyer, chances are your guests will, too. Make sure there are definite pathways that lead guests where you want them to go. If there is a part of the house that you would like to place off limits, consider placing a screen of house plants to block the path in an attractive way. If you want your guests to grab a drink and head out to the back porch, place the food at their final destination!

Order necessary supplies: Don't make the mistake of assuming that you either have to buy a ton of dinner plates or just use paper. Do what party planners do! They rent. It is very reasonable to rent the dishes and glassware you need. Best of all, some rental places don't require that you clean the dishes before returning them. Consider renting tables and chairs if you don't have enough. Delivery, set up, and pick up can also be arranged.

Figure out the decorations: Stand outside your front door and pretend to be arriving for the party. What would make you excited? Plan on decorating the door to enhance the anticipation of entering. Next, think about the serving areas and what to put on them. Create centerpieces that are big enough to make a statement but leave enough room for the food!

THREE DAYS TO GO

Check out the lighting plan: Figure out how to set the mood properly. Check whether or not you have the appropriate illumination. Consider stringing lights around a fireplace mantel or door frames. Candles can also add ambience. Make sure you have matches!

Get the refrigerator ready: Take a few minutes to make some room in the refrigerator. Empty out leftovers and reorganize to fit your larger platters, or at least make room for your new shopping. This isn't a task you want to do when you have five bags of groceries to unload.

Shop for all the food and drinks, excluding ice: Since the menu and theme have been established, keep it simple.

Prepare what you can: Cook what can be made ahead of time. Think of foods that can be frozen and reheated the day of the party, like lasagna.

Don't clean the house: It sounds crazy, but picking up is the most you are going to do. Don't do any heavy cleaning. Now is not the time to throw your back out mopping for two hours. Do clean the toilets, sinks, and vacuum the floors in the bathrooms that will be used by your guests. Tidy up by picking up stray objects. Just before a party, I use an empty clothes basket. I just go room to room and pick up anything that isn't where it's supposed to be. These things can be dealt with later. You have a party to throw!

THE DAY BEFORE THE PARTY

Set up the bar: Assemble all the drink ingredients. Put out wine buckets. Set out separate coolers, one for drinks, and one for ice. Refrigerate all drinks that need to be chilled.

Set up the buffet area: Putting a little thought into the arrangement of the food makes the party seem professionally done. Place all the serving trays and bowls in their prospective spots on the buffet table. Determine a pleasing arrangement for them. Larger bowls should go in back. Place some books under the tablecloth to "build up" pedestals for the bowls in the back. Make sure you wrap the books with a plastic garbage bag to protect them from accidental spills. However, be realistic. You won't be able to set up your buffet if you are using your kitchen table, but at least make a plan.

Create place cards: If you are serving a formal dinner, you should know your final count by now. Hand-write the place cards and think through where you want people to sit at your table. I know that place cards sound corny, but they take away the "jockeying for the best seat" moment, and will make your party run smoother. Besides, shouldn't you sit with who you want, and not be stuck with a bad spot at the table?

THE DAY OF THE PARTY

Final preparations to food: Assemble salads and store in the refrigerator. Marinate meats no more than six hours in advance. Start any last-minute cooking at least three hours before the party. Leave time to relax and shower before your guests arrive.

Set up the tables and chairs: If you've ordered items to be delivered, make sure someone is home to receive them. Arrange the centerpieces. Put out all serving pieces with utensils in the spots where you want them. Then set the table or lay out your final buffet.

Empty the dishwasher: It's very important to start working in the kitchen with an empty dishwasher. As you prep one or two of the last items on your menus, use the rinse cycle to eliminate dishwashing.

Put final touches on the bar: Pick up ice and put it in a cooler, ready to serve. Make sure you have napkins and glasses stationed by the beverages.

Pick up one last time: Do a last-minute sweep and gather up any stray items that have migrated in the last 24 hours. Clutter needs to be stowed away and counter space free so it can be used to its maximum capacity.

Pre-fill the coffeemaker: If you serve coffee, offer a choice between regular and decaffeinated. Borrow a neighbor's extra coffeemaker if you don't have a second one. Serving tea is also a nice option.

Setting Up a Bar

The rules for the bar go as follows: Make it easy to get a drink and don't run out! You may be tempted to hire a bartender, but in the keep-it-simple approach, this just isn't necessary. Instead, you can offer a limited choice of pre-made mixed drinks, like sangria or martinis, and place them in a glass pitcher. If you are serving specialty drinks, a fun way to list them is to make a drink list. Get a picture frame and stand, write out a menu, and display it on the bar. Limit the choices to two types of specialty drinks so it's not a big decision to make.

A bar can be made from any type of table, just make sure it's easy for everyone to get to. Place it far enough from a wall so that someone can stand behind it. Dress it up with fabric or tablecloth in theme colors. Place a small container, like a copper bucket or fun colored plastic bin, on the table and fill it with ice. Open two or three bottles of wine so that everyone can get a drink easily. Put the rest of the wine behind the table.

When serving mixed drinks, line up all the bottles so that guests can view the choices. Make sure to have many non-alcoholic alternatives. A standard in our house is a non-alcoholic cocktail of seltzer, cranberry juice, and a squeeze of lime. You can also offer sparkling water, a variety of sodas, and plain, uncarbonated water in a pitcher with lemon slices.

The glassware at the bar needs to reflect what you are serving. Don't panic and think you need an entire collection of specialty glasses for every cocktail imaginable. Nobody expects that. Instead, stick with the basics. You could easily get away with a 6-ounce wine glass for both red and white wine; a short, fat glass for mixed drinks; and a tall, thin glass for sparkling water, juice, soda, or beer. A funky, large goblet can stand in for frozen drinks.

Garnishes finish out a bar. Lemons, limes, cherries, oranges, olives, and cocktail onions are all typical bar garnishes. Cut lemons and limes into wedges, slices, and peels before the party. Have a stack of dishtowels, trash bags, and extra ice on hand, including a trash can nearby as well. It's also nice to include a salty bowl of nuts or pretzels near the bar, but only if you want people to linger there.

More Than Your Typical Drink Glasses

Here are some extra glasses you can have on hand.

Beer mug: A round cylinder with a long handle. Thick glass insulates and maintains the drink temperature.

Hurricane glass: An hourglass-shaped glass with a stem used for specialty drinks.

Highball: An 8- to 10-ounce tall, thin glass, used for juice-based cocktails like Bloody Marys.

Margarita glass: Wide-mouthed glass that narrows in a curve to the stem, and can also be used for frozen drinks like daiquiris.

Martini glass: An inverted cone on a tall, thin stem, used for martini-style drinks.

Old-Fashioned glass: A short, wide glass used for mixed drinks, fruit juices, and single liquors when serving vodka or Scotch.

Index

prep zone, 80–81

pressure cooker, 192

produce, 143–146

project log, 3, 47

Q

quartz, manufactured, 23

R

ranges, 51

recipes

    choosing, 182

    cookbooks, 196–198

    measuring, 193–195

    organizing, 93–94

    substitutions, 195–196

reduction, 187

refrigerator, 42–44

    cleaning of, 128–129

    organizing, 90–92

regional cuisine, 139-142, 149, 198

rice cooker, 57

roasting, 190

S

salts, 173–174

sauces, 187–188

sautéing, 186–187

searing, 186

seasoning mixes, 174–176

seat cushions, 115–116

serving tray decoration, 112–113

silicone bakeware, 65–66

silver, polishing, 133

silverware (flatware), 77–78, 208

simmering, 185

sinks, cleaning, 127–128

slow cooker, 57, 192–193

smoking point, 177

solid-surface countertops, 23–25

space planner, 9

spices, 82–83, 170–176

sponges, 121

stainless steel cookware, 61, 63, 64

stainless steel countertops, 28

steaming, 186

stewing, 186

stocks, 165

stone countertops, 21–23

stone floors, 34–35, 126

stones, sharpening, 74

stoneware, 65

storage systems, 92–93

style

    cabinets, 12–16, 18–20

    choosing, 10–11

    Contemporary, 13–15

    countertops, 20–31

    Country, 12–13

    Eclectic, 16

    flooring, 33–38

    focal point, 11–12, 20, 98

    lighting, 39–40

    plumbing fixtures, 31–32

    Traditional, 12

sugars, 179

syrups, 179

T

task lighting, 40

Thermafoil, 18, 19

tile countertops, 29

tile floors, 35,126

toaster ovens, 55, 132

Photo Credits